D1621258

EMPERORS OF
THE RISING SUN

EMPERORS
OF THE
RISING SUN

THREE BIOGRAPHIES

Stephen S. Large

KODANSHA INTERNATIONAL
Tokyo • New York • London

Photo Credits:
The publisher wishes to thank the following for providing photo-
graphic material: Kyodo Tsushinsha, Asahi Shinbunsha, Mainichi
Shinbunsha, Yomiuri Shinbunsha, and the Imperial Household
Agency.

Distributed in the United States by Kodansha America, Inc.,
114 Fifth Avenue, New York N.Y. 10011, and in the United
Kingdom and continental Europe by Kodansha Europe Ltd.,
95 Aldwych, London WC2B 4JF. Published by Kodansha
International Ltd., 17-14 Otowa 1-chome, Bunkyo-ku, Tokyo
112, and Kodansha America, Inc.

CONTENTS

PREFACE

My broad purpose in this book is to introduce Emperors Meiji (Mutsuhito), Taishō (Yoshihito), and Shōwa (Hirohito). Surprisingly, there is no focused study in English of either Meiji or Taishō. More has been written on Emperor Shōwa,[1] but as far as I am aware this is the first work to consider Hirohito in a comparative light alongside his grandfather and father, with a view to identifying major continuities and discontinuities across their respective reigns.

It is generally true, as the German physician Erwin Baelz wrote, that to his subjects the Japanese emperor "is not so much an individual as the incarnation of an idea"—of nationhood.[2] Or, as the Englishman William Elliot Griffis expressed it, "The ruler of Everlastingly Great Japan is expected to be less a personality than a sacred figurehead."[3] Yet, to Japanese and foreigners who dealt with them directly, Japan's first three modern emperors were not just abstract symbols. Each was distinctive in terms of outlook, personality, temperament, and political style. In this necessarily brief account, I hope to show what they were like in private and public life, their strengths and weaknesses, how they reacted to the crises they faced, and their overall significance in modern Japanese history.

The eventful reign of Emperor Meiji from 1867 to 1912 is

well-known for the Meiji Restoration of 1868, the subsequent centralization of state power, the advent in 1889 of constitutional government, and the emergence of Japan as a growing industrial and imperial power in Asia. In the emperor cult that was gradually built up around him, Meiji vividly symbolized the nation's pride in these achievements. While it is indisputable that he was widely venerated as a powerful ruler and "manifest deity" (*arahitogami*), the question remains of just how important Meiji was in the political and military history of his era. Other interesting questions concerning Meiji revolve around the fact that he was born in 1852, when the Tokugawa shogunate still held sway, and had to adjust to a great many changes in Japan's quest for a modern political form. This inevitably led to strains in his personal life as he endeavored to cope with the complexities and ambiguities of his office. We will see that very much the same was true of his successors, Taishō and Shōwa.

Emperor Taishō reigned from 1912 to 1926. During this period Japan's participation on the Allied side in World War I enhanced its international status as a great power. Domestically, political power gradually shifted from a small circle of "elder statesmen" (*genrō*), who had predominated since the Restoration, to an increasingly robust party movement against a background of rising social and political ferment. Taishō himself, burdened by illness, insecurity, and unfavorable comparisons with his more illustrious father, was notably unsuited for the role of emperor and ultimately drifted into complete political obscurity after the appointment of his son, Crown Prince Hirohito, as regent (*sesshō*) in November 1921. Still, was Taishō the mad fool that many accounts suggest, and to what extent was the creation of the Taishō Regency the result of a palace coup, bearing important implications for the monarchy in the 1920s? After Taishō's "retirement" in 1921, the focus of my chapter on him shifts to Hirohito's little-known career as regent, which is discussed further in the ensuing chapter.

While Taishō is the least known of Japan's modern emperors, though the most colorful, Emperor Shōwa is by far the best known, though relatively stiff and bland. In part Hirohito's greater familiarity stems from the unusual length of his reign, from late 1926 to early 1989. During this time Japan experienced the Great Depression, war with China and then with the Western Allies, defeat and the loss of the empire, an unprecedented foreign occupation, recovery, and the transition into the economic superpower that it is today. That he endured these many vicissitudes made it seem that Shōwa was as permanently fixed on the Japanese scene as Mount Fuji.

Shōwa's historical prominence is primarily due to the intense controversies, which continue today, concerning his responsibility for war, culminating in the 1941–45 "Greater East Asian War," as the Japanese referred to World War II in Asia. With this in mind I have chosen to emphasize the dramatic early decades of his reign, through the Occupation.

As in the case of Emperor Meiji, there is a need to distinguish myths from realities in studying Shōwa, who in many ways embodied the puzzling contradictions of twentieth-century Japan. The key questions are: how far, and to what ends, was he directly involved in the political decisions that led to aggression and war from 1931 to 1945? If his intervention proved decisive in ending the war in 1945, why was he unable to prevent war in 1941? And, what did his survival on the throne, as "symbol emperor" (*shōchō tennō*), mean for Japan's postwar history? This last question touches on the historical legacy of Shōwa to Heisei, the reign of the present emperor, Akihito.[4]

Before turning to my narrative, I would like to make some general observations concerning the emperors' political context down to 1945. The term "emperor" (in Japanese, *tennō*; literally, "heavenly sovereign") suggests the arbitrary power of a Caesar, Tsar, or Kaiser. But the emperors did not act as political free agents. For one thing, they were constrained by their advisers at court and by other government officials in a system of oligarchical rule which has been aptly described as a "bureaucratic monarchy."[5] For another, they were constrained by the ambiguous definition of their powers in the Meiji constitution. Promulgated in 1889, the constitution provided for both absolute and limited monarchy; some articles gave the emperor vast prerogatives while others stipulated that the exercise of these prerogatives was the responsibility of ministers of state. Thus, although sovereignty clearly resided in the emperor, such was the confusion in interpreting his constitutional prerogatives that no one, least of all the emperors themselves, knew for sure how far they could go in asserting the powers the constitution ascribed to them.

The emperors were also constrained by expectations concerning their role as "manifest deities," whose sacred authority harked back in Shintō mythology to the Sun Goddess, Amaterasu. Their chief political function was to legitimize the policies of the government—whether or not they personally agreed with them—by ritually sanctioning them with the formal "imperial will," much as Japanese emperors had always done. Indeed, the imperial house law, dating from 1889, in effect provided for the autonomy of the imperial house from the government precisely in order to maintain the transcendental, sacred authority of the throne as the source of political legitimation.

Moreover, the emperors were limited politically by the long-standing belief, adopted from ancient Chinese precedents, that government was based on "imperial virtue" and that, accordingly, "The sceptre should not be shown. For its inner nature is non-assertion."[6] That is, a benevolent emperor himself need not govern; this was the task of his ministers, whom he appointed to office and who, under the Meiji constitution, were politically responsible for affairs of state. However, the traditional notion of government founded upon imperial virtue strongly implied that the emperor was nonetheless morally responsible for what the government did in his name. This consideration, too, constrained Emperors Meiji, Taishō, and Shōwa.

These constraints were reinforced by others, including the elaborations of court ritual and protocol as well as the imperatives of the public role demanded by the emperor cult—that of an august "manifest deity" who stood symbolically "above the clouds." Taken together, they were likely to make Japan's modern emperors more politically cautious than bold. In the last analysis, how far a given emperor would assert himself or resist constraints upon his powers depended essentially upon his own personality, temperament, political style, and political outlook. This is why it is best to see Japan's modern emperors not solely as "incarnations" of an idea or as "sacred figureheads" but also as individuals whose political choices reflected the distinctive personal attributes they brought to the throne.

Yet, limited as their powers might have been, the emperors potentially had considerable political influence owing to the informal process of "working through the court," whereby Japan's ruling elite strove to declare the formal imperial will for a given policy. It was behind the scenes at court that an emperor could make his mark on national events by exerting informal imperial influence as a member of the ruling elite. Here again, his personality, character, political judgment, and political skill could make a difference one way or another, especially in times of crisis.

Informal imperial influence was typically welcomed by other elites in this process of "working through the court," if only to ensure consensus on divisive issues. This made the emperor's capacity to referee conflict, and thereby hold the government together, the litmus test of his effectiveness in government. Then, too, the stakes of his participation with other elites in declaring the formal imperial will were very high for him personally. To reiterate, Meiji and Shōwa in particular knew all too well that ultimately any policy they formally ratified would be carried out in their name; they knew they would be held, in part at least, historically accountable.

There is much we do not know, and may never know, about Japan's modern emperors. Many documents which might have illuminated their careers were destroyed by Allied bombing in World War II or by Japanese officials for reasons of their own. Valuable information is also veiled by the "chrysanthemum curtain," which Japanese authorities have always used to shield the emperors from public scrutiny and criticism. Whereas students of an English monarch can study personal letters and other papers, research on Japan's emperors is hindered by limited access to crucial sources of this kind. One must work with mirrors, as it were, using indirect evidence found in the diaries, memoirs, or private papers of high court officials and ladies-in-waiting, government leaders, military men, and foreign observers. These sources, however, are often incomplete, contradictory, and subject to quite different interpretations. Needless to say, the interpretations in this book are very much my own and I alone am responsible for them.

I would like to thank Michael Brase, who invited me to write this book, and his colleagues at Kodansha International for their kind assistance, and to express my deep appreciation to my wife, Kerstin, and my colleagues in Japanese Studies at the University of Cambridge for their moral support. It is with great pleasure that I dedicate the book to the memory of my grandmother, Neva Belle Large.

Conventions
In this book Japanese names are rendered in the proper Japanese order, with the surname preceding the given name. The emperors themselves had only given names but for the most part I have followed the Japanese custom of referring to a deceased emperor according to his formal reign name, e.g., Meiji, Taishō, or Shōwa. Macrons, which indicate long vowels in Japanese, have been employed throughout except in the case of such well-known place names as Tokyo, Kyoto, and Osaka.

MEIJI
(MUTSUHITO)

•

The "Restored" Emperor

Emperor Meiji in his prime.

One of the first foreign impressions of Emperor Meiji was recorded by Algernon Mitford, who was present when Meiji, then fifteen years of age, met the British minister to Japan, Sir Harry Parkes, in Osaka on March 26, 1868. Meiji had become the 122nd emperor of Japan on January 9, 1867, following the death by smallpox of his father, Emperor Kōmei (Osahito). The Restoration had been proclaimed as recently as January 3, 1868, by anti-Tokugawa loyalists at the imperial court in Kyoto. Later that month the loyalist forces of Chōshū and Satsuma had achieved a decisive victory in the battle of Toba-Fushimi, which ensured the downfall of the Tokugawa shogunate even though the civil war would continue sporadically until the last Tokugawa resistance was overcome in August 1869. When Mitford first saw the emperor, the new reign name had not yet been formally designated "Meiji," or "enlightened rule." That occurred in September 1868.

To Mitford, Meiji looked more like the king of a traditional, old society than the sovereign of a future new state. He later recalled that Meiji was "a tall youth with a bright eye and clear complexion: his demeanor was very dignified…. He was dressed in a white coat with long padded trousers of crimson silk trailing like a lady's court-train." Atop his hat was "a long, stiff, flat plume of black gauze" and his "eyebrows were shaved off and painted in high up on his forehead; his cheeks were rouged and his lips painted with red and gold. His teeth were blackened" in the traditional manner of the imperial court. During his prepared speech, Meiji expressed due respect for the Queen and told Parkes he hoped for friendly relations between their two countries. This augured well for the future, Mitford noted, now that the Tokugawa policy of seclusion had been abandoned. But concerning Meiji himself Mitford observed, "As might be expected from his extreme youth and the novelty of the situation to one who had only recently left the women's apartments, the Mikado showed some symptoms of shyness. He hardly spoke above a whisper, so the words were repeated aloud by the Prince of the Blood on his right side…."[1]

Nearly twenty years later Meiji made a quite different impression on the young Clara Whitney, the daughter of an English educator, when she met him on April 25, 1884, at a party in Tokyo for the foreign legations and Japanese nobles. Dressed in a French military uniform, he had "rather heavy features, a slight goatee and mustache and a very pleasant mild expression on his face. He shook hands with the ministers and their ladies, bowed graciously and smiled." When a German countess bowed before him, "I caught a half-amused, half-puzzled expression on His Majesty's face as he looked down at the mass of silk and fluffy lace."[2]

The awkwardness Meiji had displayed to Mitford in 1868

had by now given way to a more confident public demeanor, and he seemed at home in his role as head of a modern nation state. This personal transformation owed much to Meiji's own resourcefulness, but it would have been quite inconceivable without the influence of his advisers, including the men and their protégés who ruled Japan from behind the throne after taking power in the Restoration. In a very real sense his rapid adaptation to the imperial role, which was defined and redefined in the process of building a nation state, was their collective achievement as much as it was Meiji's.

The Making of Emperor Meiji

Meiji was Emperor Kōmei's second son (the first died soon after birth). He was born in Kyoto on November 3, 1852, eight months before Commodore Matthew Perry's American squadron of "black ships" arrived in Tokyo Bay and two years prior to the first of the so-called "unequal treaties," which the Tokugawa shogunate signed with Perry in 1854. Meiji's mother, Yoshiko, a prominent court lady, was the daughter of the Great Counselor Nakayama Tadayasu. Meiji spent his childhood in the Nakayama household, for it was customary to entrust the upbringing of imperial children to an eminent court family. Nakayama thus took personal charge of Meiji's early education. Later, when Meiji became emperor, Nijō Nariyuki was appointed regent to guide him politically. But this regency, which was short-lived in any case, seems to have been only a formality. Other men would prove more influential in his political education.

As a boy, Meiji lived in a sheltered world. He and his playmates—children selected from aristocratic families, like

Prince Saionji Kinmochi, who would come to dominate the court in the late Taishō and early Shōwa periods—were constantly supervised by ladies-in-waiting (*nyokan*), who attended them day and night. He was "little more than a prisoner in a golden cage."[3] Evidently a physically delicate, rather effeminate child, he nonetheless liked to play with wooden swords and to ride a wooden hobby horse while shouting at the top of his lungs. Spoiled by his attendants and perhaps frustrated by his confined existence, he was often irritable and spoke harshly to anyone who prevented him from having his way. This hot-tempered wilfulness, which continued into adulthood, made Meiji an exception to the traditional observation that, owing to the emphasis on precedent and protocol, "The training of imperial children bred in them habits of docility and rigidly patterned behavior."[4]

In 1860 Meiji was given the name Mutsuhito (he had been previously named Prince Suke, or Suke-no-miya) and was formally made heir to the throne. By then, prominent court nobles, including Prince Iwakura Tomomi and Prince Sanjō Sanetomi, were largely responsible for his personal affairs. Later, they would be instrumental in arranging his marriage, in February 1869, to Ichijō Haruko, whose father, Ichiji Tadaka, was minister of the left. She bore Meiji no children, but he reportedly visited her apartments nearly every day in what was a companionable relationship. Following her death in April 1914, she was known posthumously as Empress Shoken.

Iwakura, Sanjō, Kido Takayoshi of Chōshū, and other key figures in the new Restoration regime drafted Meiji's first rescripts and edicts. An early example was the well-known

Charter Oath, an imperial declaration dated April 6, 1868, which pledged among other things that "Knowledge shall be sought throughout the world so as to strengthen the foundations of imperial rule." That Meiji had not ventured beyond Kyoto until his tour in March that year to Osaka (where Mitford first saw him) indicates how far Meiji himself had to go in overcoming the parochialism of his early years.

It was not until the autumn of 1868 that his own world expanded significantly. Following the government's decision to make Tokyo (formerly Edo, the shōgun's capital) the seat of the new imperial regime, Meiji travelled overland with a large retinue of 3,300 attendants on his first visit to Tokyo. Along the way he viewed the open sea for the first time, which prompted Kido Takayoshi, who accompanied him, to record in his diary: "I was moved to tears by the realization that this marks the beginning of an era in which His Majesty's influence will become worldwide."[5] When the imperial proccession reached Tokyo on November 26, "a multitude, in the tens of thousands, lined both sides of the road to pay their respects" as Meiji's palanquin, surmounted by a golden phoenix, passed by on its way to the former shogunal palace, where he would stay.[6] He briefly returned to Kyoto in January 1869 before his permanent relocation to Tokyo two months later.

The de facto leaders of the new government, in particular Ōkubo Toshimichi and Saigō Takamori from Satsuma, had relocated Meiji to Tokyo chiefly to free him from the conservative ethos of Kyoto. Subsequently, in 1871 Saigō introduced reforms, first, to reduce the number of ladies-in-waiting who attended the emperor, on the grounds that hitherto they had exercised too much influence, and second, to enable people

opposed but finally gave in

from a samurai as opposed to an aristocratic background to be appointed to high posts at court. It was a mark of his conservative upbringing that for a time Meiji himself strenuously opposed these reforms, which he finally approved in 1872.

Meiji soon developed an especially close relationship with Saigō, who encouraged him to develop his physical strength by going horseback riding and to take an interest in military affairs as commander-in-chief of the armed forces. Meiji enjoyed reviewing the troops, most of whom were from Chōshū and Satsuma, comprising the *goshinpei*, or the imperial bodyguard, established in April 1871. His personal affection for Saigō would survive Saigō's participation in the abortive 1877 Satsuma Rebellion, in which he was shot and killed;[7] Meiji pardoned Saigō posthumously, as indeed he pardoned Tokugawa Keiki (Yoshinobu), the last shōgun.

After Saigō's death, Meiji apparently became bored with his military duties. From 1877 to the early 1890s, to the disappointment of Yamagata Aritomo, the principal advocate of Japan's military modernization, Meiji frequently refused to attend the biannual grand military maneuvers.[8] His indifference towards military matters ended when Japan went to war with China in 1894.

In the early 1870s, the "Sat-Chō" (Satsuma and Chōshū) oligarchs who dominated the new regime gradually consolidated the authority of the central government. They abolished the domains in favor of prefectures, eliminated the long-standing privileges of the samurai and, ultimately, their existence as a class by introducing compulsory military conscription, and undertook other, similarly sweeping measures. Meiji was indispensable to this process of political centralization as the symbol of a new national consciousness. This was a time when loyalties were still more focused on the former Tokugawa domains than on the country as a whole, and when there was still no little resistance to the authority of the new Meiji state. But before he could serve this purpose government leaders knew that he had to be "sold" to the people, many of whom were scarcely aware of the imperial house, not to mention the young emperor himself. Accordingly, Ōkubo Toshimichi insisted that Meiji should go on tour, beginning with his trip to Osaka in 1868, as a means of rallying popular support for the new regime. Altogether, during his reign of forty-five years Meiji went on 102 imperial excursions (*gyōkō*) to all parts of Japan, seventy of which took place before 1889. The most important were his six Great Circuits (the term recalls the tours of the Chinese sovereign during the ancient Chou dynasty) in 1872, 1876, 1878, 1880, 1881, and 1885.

In the first instance the idea behind these tours was to project Meiji as an ideal Confucian monarch whose reign would be based on "imperial virtue," or benevolent compassion toward his subjects. The tours were also meant to educate Meiji for this role while fostering his general sense of political responsibility. That he was not yet sufficiently attentive to national political affairs worried Japan's elites. In May 1874, Kido admonished him, "You must, Your Majesty, exert yourself more than ever to fulfill your divinely appointed task." On another occasion, eager that he should confer with his ministers on controversial political issues, Kido and Prince Sanjō Sanetomi felt obliged to advise Meiji, "We want Your Majesty, therefore, to demand explanations in person from the Senior Ministers and other officials for actions contrary to the

•
23
•

Imperial intent, and to inquire in each instance about that which Your Majesty has doubts."[9] Even during the Satsuma Rebellion, which represented the greatest challenge to the government since the Restoration, Kido deemed it necessary to tell Meiji that he should "go to the Imperial Study every day to receive the daily reports on the state of the battlefront and other matters."[10]

The second of Meiji's Great Circuits, his northern tour in 1876, is a fairly typical illustration of what these expeditions involved. It lasted from June 2, when he departed overland from Tokyo, until his return by ship from Hokkaidō on July 20. Much of the time Meiji rode a horse along roads that were no more than dirt tracks; otherwise he was carried by palanquin or traveled in a horse-drawn carriage. At Nikkō, he visited the shrine to the first Tokugawa shōgun, Ieyasu. There and at other historical spots, such as Sendai, the former seat of the Date domain, he heard lectures by members of his entourage on his country's rich past.

He met the governor and other high officials of each prefecture he visited and was briefed about local crafts, industries, crops, social and economic issues, and health problems, such as the high prevalence of beriberi in some regions and of various eye ailments in others. Frequently, these reports came at the end of a very hectic day: for instance, on July 7 in Morioka, after he had inspected the criminal and civil courts, schools, a cocoonery, a silk filature mill, a horse-breeding station, and had observed a traditional dance performed by local farmers. Wherever he went he was greeted along the road by throngs of schoolchildren and other curious onlookers, for whom the emperor had been either entirely unknown or a

legendary personage who existed above the mundane world of human affairs. They sometimes collected the soil where he had stood, as if to preserve his magical presence after he had departed. Prefectural authorities, the owners of new enterprises, school principals, and the like were grateful to receive donations of money for the building of new roads, factories, and schools. This kind of imperial benevolence on behalf of public works and good causes, including relief funds for the victims of fires, earthquakes, typhoons, and famine, would typify Meiji's reign and that of his successors.

Through his first northern tour, and the many others that followed, Meiji learned firsthand about his realm while his subjects increasingly identified with him as their sovereign and, through him, with Japan as a nation state. During this tour, Meiji began to discover how rigorous his role could be as head of state, and he often showed signs of fatigue, boredom and indifference. According to Kido's diary entry for June 19, he and Prince Iwakura privately discussed "our deep concern about the Emperor's development. I sincerely hoped that His Majesty would make greater progress during this tour." Similarly, on July 2 he wrote, "In recent days I have put myself to a good deal of trouble, and tried in several ways to educate the Emperor as to what he is seeing." Iwakura "also endeavored to admonish His Majesty as to what to do," apparently to no avail. That very evening, however, Meiji surprised them by talking "without pause" about "the merits and demerits of the things he had observed, so that I felt most grateful."[11]

Nevertheless, in a later entry Kido reports a conversation with Iwakura and Imperial Household Minister Tokudaiji Sanenori: "As the Emperor's return to Tokyo is nearing, I

Concerns his
political
understanding

spoke without reserve … of my deep concern about the need
for more careful assistance to the Emperor on political matters, based on what I have observed while attending him on
this Imperial tour."[12] After the deaths in 1877 of Kido, due to
illness, and Saigō, and the assassination of Ōkubo in 1878, a
new group of men would "assist" Meiji: Motoda Eifu (Naga-
zane), Itō Hirobumi (from Chōshū), and later Yamagata
Aritomo (also from Chōshū). Of these men, Motoda was at
first the most influential in cultivating Meiji's sense of political responsibility based on Confucian values. After his appointment in 1871 as lecturer to Meiji on Chinese books,
Motoda personally introduced him to the great classics of the
Confucian canon, including the *Analects* of Confucius, the
Doctrine of the Mean, and the *Book of History*. Motoda would
explain these books to Meiji "until I was certain that he believed firmly. His Majesty was extremely fond of these discussions and always listened carefully. I never noticed him to
become tired of them."[13]

To be sure, in the 1870s and 1880s, the popular slogan "civilization and enlightenment" (*bunmei kaika*) encouraged enthusiasm for Western learning, and what was known as
"*teiōgaku*" ("learning for the emperor") included a strong variety of Western subjects as well as Eastern learning. The Confucian scholar Nishimura Shigeki, for instance, lectured Meiji
on French law and world history, and Katō Hiroyuki, a leading proponent of Western studies, had Meiji read Fukuzawa
Yukichi's famous books about the author's firsthand observations of the West, as well as Japanese translations of Samuel
Smiles' *Self-Help* and J. K. Bluntschli on Western constitutional systems. Meiji also studied German for a time, albeit

without mastering it. This Western orientation in Meiji's education led him in 1871 to endorse enthusiastically the Iwakura mission, the aim of which was to study the sources of wealth and power in the West. Meiji himself would have undertaken an imperial tour of Europe had this proposal not been blocked by conservatives at court in 1886.

However, Meiji's lecturer on the Confucian classics, Motoda Eifu, had little use for Western learning, not to mention Western lifestyles, and this attitude rubbed off on Meiji, at least to the extent of making him somewhat ambivalent about Western influences. In 1884, for example, Meiji unsuccessfully opposed the appointment of Itō Hirobumi as imperial household minister, fearing that Itō, who enthusiastically advocated European-style dress and such activities as ballroom dancing when entertaining Western dignitaries, would indiscriminately introduce Western ways at the imperial court itself.[14] Similarly, after inspecting Tokyo Imperial University in October 1886, Meiji complained to Motoda that so great was the university's preoccupation with law, science, and other applied subjects that it entirely neglected the study of moral (that is, Confucian) values.

Owing to Motoda's influence, Meiji was perhaps the most Confucian-minded of Japan's modern emperors. In particular, he believed that he, as emperor, should personify the Confucian principles of filial piety, benevolence, and compassion, all of which typified the ideal sage-king in the East Asian classical tradition. Motoda, going one step further, thought that the emperor should rule, not just reign, on the basis of imperial virtue, and relatedly, that there should be no separation between the imperial court and the government. As we will see, things did not turn out this way. Yet Motoda did impress upon Meiji the conviction that the emperor was morally responsible for political affairs. Thus, when Meiji pardoned the last Tokugawa rebels in late 1869, his edict stated, "In Our opinion, the unnatural condition of rebellion depends solely on the possession, or want, of kingly virtue in the Sovereign."[15]

This same notion of overall moral responsibility may explain Meiji's response to the "Ōtsu Incident" of May 1891, when the Russian Crown Prince Nicholas, then in Japan on a state visit, was stabbed by a deranged Japanese policeman. When informed of the matter, Meiji at once insisted upon going personally by train to Kyoto to apologize to the Crown Prince, who was recovering from his wounds at an inn. Meiji then accompanied Nicholas to Kobe and had dinner with him on board the Crown Prince's ship. Itō Hirobumi made it clear in a subsequent interview that these gestures of imperial sympathy were initiated by Meiji, not by the government.[16]

More generally, the shared belief that state and society should be based on Confucian principles explains why Meiji was pleased to endorse Motoda's draft of the Imperial Rescript on Education, which Meiji promulgated on October 30, 1890. Partly intended to prevent the people from being led astray by Western ideas, and partly to anchor the nation against the approaching swells of constitutional government, this rescript included the well-known passage, "Ye, Our subjects, be filial to your parents, affectionate to your brothers and sisters; as husbands and wives be harmonious, as friends true; bear yourselves in modesty and moderation; extend your benevolence to all ... advance public good and promote common interests." At Meiji's insistence, the rescript also admonished the people

to "respect the Constitution and observe the laws," but its main thrust was to make Confucian ethics the foundation of public morality in Japan. Much the same evocation of Confucian values is seen in Meiji's later Boshin rescript, issued in 1908, which aimed to promote loyalty, thrift, and hard work as a means of ensuring social cohesion amidst signs of growing class conflict.

Until his death in 1891, Motoda Eifu continued to advise Meiji on political as well as moral issues. Yet it was chiefly in his role as moral preceptor that Motoda gave Meiji "confidence in himself and principles to proceed by."[17] By then, Meiji had come to take his political duties very seriously indeed, and he faced new challenges in Japan's transition to constitutional government. Rather than standing in tension with modernity, the Confucian tradition evoked by Motoda helped Meiji to adapt to the roles required of him as a modern monarch.

However, the "making of Emperor Meiji" went far beyond the efforts of Motoda and others to "Confucianize" the emperor, so to speak. It also encompassed the public invention of Meiji as a multifaceted national symbol, with the result that from the 1890s he became the focus of an increasingly powerful emperor cult propagated by the government, the media, the schools, the military, and later the shrines comprising State Shintō. The intention, and in significant measure the overall effect, of making Meiji the supreme icon of modern Japanese nationalism and its underpinning native traditions, was to mobilize the people's loyalty to the state and to persuade them to sacrifice their labor and if necessary their lives for the sake of building a "wealthy country, strong army"

(*fukoku kyōhei*) in competition with the West.

To illustrate the emperor's growing symbolic preeminence, Meiji was honored on national festival days, including his birthday (November 3) and Kigensetsu (February 11), when the Japanese commemorated the accession to the throne of Jimmu, the first emperor. On these occasions, school children and members of the armed forces were encouraged to bow before photographs of the emperor and to sing the national anthem, "Kimi ga yo," the words of which suggested the eternal nature of imperial rule. The designation of imperial reign names similarly implied that a period of time itself was the emperor's to possess, while various imperial terms, such as *tennō* ("heavenly sovereign"), *heika* ("His Majesty," hence *tennō heika*), and *banzai* ("Long live the Emperor"), connoted an authority and power that transcended the mundane world of humankind. In addition, Meiji and the imperial house were honored by popular pilgrimages to the grand shrines at Ise and Izumo, which were associated with important episodes in the legend of Amaterasu and her divine progeny, as well as to Yasukuni Shrine, which was built near the imperial palace in 1869 to house the spirits of Japan's war dead in the service of the emperor.

Consequently, well before his death in 1912, Meiji symbolized not only the nation's progress towards the goals of modern "civilization," empire, and constitutional government, but also the *kokutai*, or "national polity," in which the emperor, the people, and the land of the gods were allegedly united in both time and space. Hence he was venerated as the chief priest of Japan who performed sacred Shintō rites at the palace shrine to propitiate the gods and guarantee a bountiful

harvest every year. The notion, advocated by conservative ide-
ologues, that he was a "manifest deity" meant that his subjects
were not supposed to look at him directly, and certainly not
down upon him, as he passed by. Nor, for the same reason,
were his doctors and nurses allowed to touch him. Even his
rescripts were seen to have an oracular authority that commanded the greatest possible respect: to mispronounce a word
or phrase when reading these texts aloud on solemn ceremonial occasions could well result in charges of lese majesty.

It is difficult to distinguish Meiji the man among these
many layers of imperial symbolism, but one can well imagine
that it was no easy thing for Meiji, or indeed for Emperors
Taishō and Shōwa, to live with, and up to, the myths and
mystique which gradually adhered to the high office of emperor. As one writer states, Meiji's "artificially exalted position, the sacredness attributed to his person, and his onerous
religious and ceremonial duties, in addition to his political responsibilities, put severe strain upon him, strain that his early
training and natural inclinations had not altogether prepared
him to bear."[18]

This strain may explain why, judging from the available
sources, Meiji was a man of many paradoxes. Publicly he personified a changing Japan, but in his personal routine, as discovered by Erwin Baelz in the course of serving the imperial
family as a court physician, Meiji was "averse from all
change," as when he initially objected to moving to the newly
constructed imperial palace in January 1889. Then, again,
Meiji was publicly associated with the general promotion of
Western material life, but Baelz noted that "The Emperor's
private apartments are purely Japanese, without tables, chairs,

or beds. This shows how little the European modes of living have penetrated beneath the surface" at the palace.[19]

When going on tour Meiji symbolized Japan on the move. Yet, he personally did not much like to travel. Nor, it seems, did he like being the object of public attention whenever he appeared in imperial processions. This was Clara Whitney's perception on one such occasion: "His face was turned half towards us and his eyes were bent on the ground as if in meditation.... He seemed very tired as if he wished the people would not stare at him so hard."[20] Interestingly, although Meiji's photograph was widely revered in homes, schools, army barracks, and so on, Bōjō Toshinaga, who during his career as a court chamberlain served Emperors Meiji, Taishō, and Shōwa, relates that Meiji hated having his photograph taken.[21]

Baelz explains that Meiji's public appearances "were as few as possible, for he was of a retiring, one might almost say a shy, disposition. Unless for a full-dress parade, the laying of a foundation stone, a journey, or the like, he rarely left the palace" where "he occupied a small suite of private rooms with a garden separated by a high wall from the rest of the royal part."[22] On the other hand, if Meiji was essentially a shy and retiring person, he was also capable of great good humor on public occasions. After attending a state banquet in 1905, the British ambassador Sir Claude MacDonald wrote in a private letter that Meiji "chatted most amicably with everybody around." When some of the Japanese officials who were present "cracked jokes," this made Meiji "roar with laughter. It was a great revelation to me and one which pleased me very much for though a Mikado he seems very human."[23]

Meiji was human, too, in his immense fondness for strong

drink, which undoubtedly helped him escape the pressures of high office. Yet his habit of heavy drinking often alarmed his advisers. For instance, Kido relates that at a party in 1876, "The drinking bout was lively; some of us feared privately that the Emperor might go too far in his merriment."[24] The worry in later years that Meiji's excessive drinking was harmful to his health prompted some restraint at state banquets. In 1905 Baelz noted that "At the imperial table today I was greatly impressed to notice how much less 'sake' was drunk than in former days. Very few of the guests had their dishes replenished, whereas this used to be the rule."[25]

Perhaps sex also provided a welcome distraction from the stresses of political life, for Meiji had a vigorous sexual appetite and regularly slept with imperial concubines whose progeny were eligible to succeed to the throne until this system of imperial concubinage was ended in the Shōwa period. By far his favorite was Yanagihara Naruko, the eldest daughter of a cadet branch of the great Fujiwara family, who gave birth on August 31, 1879, to Yoshihito, Meiji's third son and later the Taishō Emperor. Altogether, Meiji fathered four other sons, all of whom died in infancy, and ten daughters (some sources indicate nine), of whom only four survived him. Meiji has been criticized for being a lustful man whose personal exploitation of women sharply contradicted his public advocacy of their social advancement through education and foreign travel.[26] This may be true from our perspective today, but at the time his sexual affairs were accepted, evidently even by the empress, as normal for an emperor.

Among his other interests, horses and poetry likewise provided personal outlets from the tensions of public life. An avid

rider who owned a great many fine horses which he rode on a special course in the palace grounds, Meiji appeared to some Western observers very awkward in the saddle, for he rode not in the upright position which they favored but, rather, hunched forward in the older Japanese style. He also liked to exercise on a large wooden hobby horse indoors, again as he had done as a child. He often attended the race track in Yokohama where he would personally hand out prizes to the winners. His enjoyment of horses also extended to dogs, especially a pet Yorkshire terrier which servants fed with pieces of ice on hot summer days.

Meiji began writing poetry when he was a boy and by the time he died he had composed no less than 90,000 poems, mostly in the *waka* genre, which reflected his love of nature, his concern for the welfare of his subjects or of servicemen at the front, and his own sense of loneliness in high office. That it was very natural for Meiji to turn to poetry for relaxation is seen in Kido Takayoshi's diary entry of June 10, 1876. While the imperial party were resting at Utsunomiya during the northern tour, Kido writes that the emperor "gave me a poetry theme from one of the eight famous sights of Nikkō—'a drenching shower'"—which Kido then used to compose a suitable verse of his own. Meiji would similarly designate the theme for the annual New Year's poetry party at the imperial court. Kido recalls that in January 1877 "The Imperial New Year's Poetry Party was held this afternoon and I submitted a poem also. The Imperial theme was 'a pine tree does not change its color.'"[27]

To Meiji, the significance of poetry transcended matters of personal taste. In 1881, he told the minister of education he

was distressed to see that school textbooks made too much of the emperors as military figures in Japanese history. He allowed that children like to read about war but he would much prefer them to know that historically, and in his own reign, the imperial house was more important for its cultural achievements and sponsorship of the peaceful arts.[28] It is uncertain how far Meiji himself was a sophisticated cultural connoisseur, or how far he was directly involved in the development of what became the impressive imperial art collection housed in the National Museum at Ueno, Tokyo. But that he enjoyed collecting fine clocks, porcelains, swords, and lacquerware reinforced the traditional ideal of the emperor as patron of high culture.

If Meiji held this cultural ideal of the imperial house, how did he regard the religious ideal, bred of Shintō mythology and increasingly emphasized in Japanese nationalist ideology, of the emperor as a "manifest deity"? It seems that he took seriously his performance of sacred Shintō rites at court, although many of these rites were not observed as rigorously as one might think.[29] But concerning the question of his supposed divinity, even the conservative historian Watanabe Ikujirō, writing in 1942 when wartime nationalist ideology was most intense, guessed that Meiji would have privately rejected his public image as a "god." What counted more for Meiji, Watanabe speculated, was to be respected as a man who was trying to cultivate a god-like virtue.[30]

In the field of politics and government also, *respect* was what Meiji sought most of all, for he was a proud, strong-willed man, just as he had been a strong-willed child. His superior status meant much to him. Once, for example, in June

1891, Meiji happened to notice that his throne—actually, a raised mat on the floor—was too low. Baelz states, "The Emperor could not endure that the Empress's throne should be as lofty as his. He wanted a higher one." But when a high official, who perhaps thought that Meiji was being petty at the expense of the empress, later "found that a thick silken mat had been smuggled beneath the Emperor's throne, he dragged it out and flung it to the corner of the room." This "naturally led to a great row" when Meiji discovered what the official had done.[31] Meiji was clearly not the kind of man who would easily accept the role of political figurehead as Japan embarked on its experiment in constitutional government.

Meiji and Constitutional Government

As the incumbent emperor in 1868, Meiji had soon discovered that the "restoration" of imperial rule that year did not mean that he himself would rule Japan, for power rested firmly with the Satsuma-Chōshū (Sat-Chō) coalition which governed in his name. The advent of constitutional government in 1889 merely reinforced this reality.

The Meiji constitution marked a new phase in the centralization of state power in Japan. In part, the constitution arose in response to vigorous demands by liberals in the burgeoning "movement for freedom and popular rights" (*jiyū minken undō*) of the 1870s for a popular assembly, where they hoped to contest the political predominance of the Sat-Chō oligarchy. Acting upon the advice of the government, Meiji issued a rescript in 1876 ordering the Genrōin (Senate) to begin the process of drafting a constitution that would be suitable for Japan. He then gave Prince Arisugawa Taruhito, president of

the Genroin, a Japanese translation of Alpheus Todd's *Parliamentary Government in England*, the two volumes of which had been published in London in 1867 and 1868, respectively.[32] This did not necessarily mean that Meiji endorsed Todd's theme—that in England the extensive royal prerogatives were exercised by ministers of state; in fact we do not know whether Meiji himself had read Todd's work. But Meiji's presentation of these books to Prince Arisugawa does reveal an early interest among Japan's leaders in exploring a variety of possible constitutional models from the contemporary West.

During the 1880s the government prepared for constitutional government by establishing a peerage in 1884, in anticipation of an appointive parliamentary upper house; a cabinet system in 1885; and a privy council in 1888, to ratify the constitution. Itō Hirobumi from Chōshū was the key figure in these developments, leading the way in the painstaking process of drafting the constitution. He served as Japan's first prime minister from 1885 to 1888 and for part of this period, from 1884 to 1887, as Imperial Household Minister. He was also president of the Privy Council when it ratified the constitution. Itō was especially crucial in assisting Meiji's adaptation to the new role of constitutional monarch. They did not always agree on political matters, as will be seen shortly, but as the years passed Meiji grew personally closer to Itō than to any of the other "elder statesmen," or *genrō*.

From the beginning, Meiji took an active interest in this process of political change. In 1879 he had an opportunity to confer with the former American president Ulysses S. Grant, who was then on a private visit to Japan. In *Meiji tennō ki* (The Chronicles of Emperor Meiji), which is an indispensable

source for any study of Meiji, there is a good account of their two-hour meeting on August 10 at the imperial palace. In brief, Meiji shook hands with Grant and invited him to state his opinions about political life in Japan. Grant replied through an interpreter that on the important question of whether Japan should have an elective assembly, while he did not presume to know whether the time had yet come for this, political parties and assemblies were common to "civilized" nations in the West. The virtue of an elective assembly, Grant said, was that it ensured that the government would take into account the will of the people and thereby attain their support: "No government, monarchical or republican, is as strong as the government that rests on the people."

However, Grant continued,

> You must always remember that privileges like this can never be recalled. When you give suffrage and representation you give them forever. Consequently in establishing such [an] assembly too great a caution cannot be taken. It is exceedingly dangerous to launch out too suddenly. You do not want to see anarchy as the result of any premature creation of an assembly. The surest way would be the slowest, approaching the result step by step, carefully educating the people as you go.[33]

There is no record of what precisely Meiji thought about all this, but it does seem he felt reassured that it was both possible and desirable for Japan to proceed, albeit cautiously, towards constitutional government. In supporting the proposal for an elected lower house, he often referred to Grant's advice dur-

ing the privy council's debates on the draft constitution.[34]

At various times in the 1880s Meiji actively intervened in politics, as if to serve notice that he expected to have an important say in government after the constitution came into effect. However, these interventions were of no avail. In the political crisis of October 1881, for instance, he tried to preserve unity within the ruling circle by restraining Itō from purging Ōkuma Shigenobu from the government. Ōkuma, who hailed from Hizen, was an outspoken critic of the Sat-Chō monopoly, and Itō considered his pro-English ideas on constitutional government to be radical. Itō finally brought Meiji around and Ōkuma was ousted from the government.[35] Similarly, in 1884, Meiji tried to influence key appointments in the military at a time when Yamagata Aritomo's "mainstream" faction was challenged by a group of "anti-mainstream" generals. Meiji backed the latter, as did Itō, hoping to balance off Yamagata's power in the army. But Meiji's will in the matter, and indeed Itō's, was ignored and Yamagata's faction prevailed.[36]

Despite these reversals, Meiji told Motoda Eifu in 1886 that although in the past ten years he had been unable to coordinate the government, he intended to do so now that the cabinet system had been established.[37] This of course pleased Motoda, but this was not included in Itō's scenario for Meiji. On the contrary, Itō introduced reforms in 1886 which limited the emperor's capacity to intervene in government affairs. Among these changes was the decision that the emperor should not attend cabinet meetings unless there was a major crisis. An ardent proponent of limited monarchy, Itō hoped to keep the emperor out of politics. His priority was to maintain

the political transcendence of the imperial house so that, untarnished by sectarian political conflict, the emperor could legitimize government policy by sanctioning it with the formal imperial will. This is why Itō wanted the Imperial House Law to accompany the constitution in February 1889,[38] effectively ensuring the separation of the court from the government.

By 1889 Itō had dissuaded Meiji from Motoda's view that the emperor should exert direct imperial rule. Still, in 1891 Meiji would boast that the "Constitution was in every respect determined by me, and must not be regarded as the work of Itō Hirobumi or others."[39] This was untrue: Itō, not Meiji, had set the pace in drafting the constitution. Perhaps Meiji intended his boast to protect Itō politically from critics of the constitution, including liberals for whom it was too conservative and conservatives for whom it was too liberal. In any case, it is significant that from May 1888 to January 1889, Meiji made a point of attending virtually all of the privy council's forty-one regular and three special sessions on the draft constitution. Moreover, he often participated in the discussions by asking specific questions for clarification, and he frequently pressed Itō for further explanation on many occasions when they met privately. He was plainly keen to see that he would have a significant role once the new constitutional order was in place.

Meiji trusted Itō's judgment in these deliberations, but he did not wish to be taken for granted. His sensitivity on this point is illustrated by an incident which took place on May 7, 1888. Itō, using Imperial Household Minister Hijikata Hisamoto as an intermediary, gave Meiji the draft of a speech he

had composed for Meiji to read at the formal opening of the privy council the next day. Meiji was furious that Itō had not consulted him beforehand. He angrily flung the paper down and ordered Hijikata to return it to Itō with a warning that now he might not attend the privy council meeting. Later, Itō apologized for his indiscretion and Meiji, who had calmed down, delivered the speech as anticipated.[40]

Opinion in the privy council was deeply divided between conservatives, who were adamantly opposed to any limitations on the emperor's prerogatives (*taiken*), and "liberals" of the "Manchester school," as Itō characterized them, who agreed with him on the need to introduce some limitations lest Japan end up with an absolute monarchy. Itō was very gratified that during the proceedings "His Majesty's judgment virtually always inclines towards progressive ideas."[41] In retrospect, Meiji could afford to be "progressive" in accepting certain limits on his prerogatives because, with conservative Prussia as Itō's chosen model for the Japanese constitution, the emperor was made head of state, the source of sovereignty, and the holder of virtually every conceivable executive, legislative, and military power.

In theory, the emperor alone appointed the government, made war and peace, concluded treaties, and, under article XI, possessed the power of supreme command over the armed forces. Concerning the bicameral Diet (parliament), he was empowered to open, close, and prorogue the Diet, to dissolve the elected lower house of representatives, and to make laws in the form of imperial ordinances. As well, his transcendental sacred authority—based on article I, "The Empire of Japan shall be reigned over and governed by a line of Emperors un-

•

41

•

broken for ages eternal," and on article III, "The Emperor is sacred and inviolable"—was supreme. The emperor was thus the "spiritual axis" of the state, as Itō expressed it.

had power in theory

To be sure, the practical exercise of Meiji's vast prerogatives was delegated, as Itō had also intended. The cabinet was responsible for exercising his executive prerogative, and all imperial ordinances and rescripts had to bear the countersignature of a minister of state (article LV). Likewise, his legislative prerogative was delegated to the Diet (article V), and in practice his control of the armed services was delegated to the army and navy ministries where military administration was concerned, and to the army and navy chiefs of staff where military preparedness and war operations were concerned. Although it was not stipulated in the constitution, the service chiefs were regarded as having the right of direct access to the emperor, to report on policies for which they sought his approval. This effectively put the chiefs beyond the control of the cabinet.

However, the limitations on the emperor's prerogatives notwithstanding, such was his exalted position in the constitution that the government could do nothing without his formal sanction, and it was probably for this reason that Meiji enthusiastically endorsed it. As the supreme arbiter of the national will, the emperor was expected to approve government policies whether or not he personally agreed with them. But the informal process of "working through the court" to declare the imperial will ensured that the emperor could influence government decisions. The distinguished historian Sakata Yoshio explains that the Meiji leadership expected the emperor to clarify points about which he had doubts by asking

imperial questions (*gokamon*) of his ministers, and that by doing so, he would come to "understand" a given policy and identify himself with it. The emperor's sanction, flowing as it did in the perception of the Meiji elites from the charisma of his "imperial virtue," reflected his moral, rather than political, responsibility, but this scarcely made it less important in a political system that depended upon the emperor for its legitimacy.[42]

From its inception, the Meiji constitution's ambiguous amalgam of absolute and limited monarchy made it a highly controversial document. For instance, the emperor's supreme command prerogative was originally intended to prevent partisan conflict in the cabinet and the Diet from intruding on matters of national security. It was not intended to give the emperor personal control of the armed forces. A serious practical problem, however, was that "there was no clear definition regarding either the scope of the right of supreme command or the person responsible for exercising it."[43] This issue, and many others concerning the emperor's prerogatives, sparked passionate debates in the late Meiji period and thereafter. Conservative thinkers such as Professor Uesugi Shinkichi of Tokyo Imperial University interpreted the constitution to mean direct imperial rule. By contrast, Professor Minobe Tatsukichi, of the same university, emphasized its provisions for limited monarchy. In his "emperor-organ theory" (*tennō kikan setsu*), Minobe argued that the emperor was an "organ," albeit the highest, of the state, whose prerogatives were significantly qualified by virtue of being delegated to other agencies. There will be frequent occasion later in this book to refer to Minobe's theory, which underscored the role of the cabinet and the Diet

in national politics. In the Taishō and early Shōwa periods, the theory attained widespread popularity among Japanese intellectuals and at the imperial court itself.

However, these problems of constitutional interpretation mostly lay in the future when Meiji promulgated the constitution on February 11, 1889, and formally convened the first session of the imperial Diet in November 1890, following the first national elections (with a very limited franchise) in July that year. The latter ceremony, which took place in a wooden building—not the present Diet Building, an impressive stone structure completed in 1936—was appropriately dignified, with Meiji solemnly reading the rescript to open the proceedings. Outside there were "dense crowds," who had watched his earlier procession from the palace with an almost "religious awe." Many Japanese believed that with the advent of constitutional government, the country had entered a bright new phase in its political development.[44]

It was also an anxious phase for both Meiji and the government. In February 1890 Meiji had asked Itō what would happen should there be serious clashes between the cabinet and the Diet.[45] The answer, as provided in the early 1890s, was a stalemate, owing to the ability of the parties in the elected lower house to reject the government's proposed budget as a means of protest. When the cabinet fell into disarray over this and other issues, Meiji frequently felt compelled to intervene behind the scenes in order to hold the cabinet together.

The problem of cabinet instability was compounded by rivalry between Itō Hirobumi and Yamagata Aritomo. As prime minister from December 1889 to May 1891, Yamagata advocated a tough line in dealing with the unexpectedly ob-

streperous parties in the lower house during the first Diet session. Political parties were anathema to Yamagata, who saw in their pursuit of sectarian interest a threat to his ideal of "transcendental," non-party government by elites who knew best what was good for Japan. However, Itō preferred pragmatic compromises with the parties, especially over the continuing problem of the national budget.

This conflict between Yamagata and Itō, which would last for many years, greatly troubled Prime Minister Matsukata Masayoshi's cabinet, from May 1891 to August 1892. Although neither Yamagata nor Itō served in this administration, each used his supporters on the cabinet to express his views. Consequently, Meiji repeatedly admonished the Matsukata cabinet to close ranks. In September 1891 he warned Matsukata, whom he regarded as a weak leader, that the persisting budgetary deadlock with the Diet would make it virtually impossible to govern the country.

The Matsukata cabinet was further unsettled in January 1892 by divided reactions to Itō's surprising proposal to form a new party that would assist the cabinet in the Diet. To this Yamagata was very strongly opposed, as was Matsukata. Even Meiji, who tended to follow Itō in seeking compromises between the cabinet and the Diet, found it hard to see how Itō's proposed party would help the cabinet. He also feared that Itō's initiative would make it more difficult to achieve consensus in Japan's continuing diplomatic campaign to revise and ultimately eliminate the "unequal treaties" with Western powers. Ultimately, Itō shelved his proposal. But, to anticipate future developments, he revived it later when he formed the Seiyūkai party in 1900. Yamagata regarded this initiative as a

betrayal of oligarchical rule, telling Meiji after being appointed prime minister in 1898, "The affairs of state would be handled competently by a politician like Itō, but without Itō's ability, I rely on your aid in the conduct of political affairs.... My interpretation of the constitution differs from that of Itō.... I am absolutely opposed to a party cabinet."[46] However, by 1900 Itō's Seiyūkai initiative had Meiji's approval, for by then the politics of confrontation had largely given way to the politics of compromise between the cabinet and the Diet.

Meiji had further cause for concern about the instability of the Matsukata cabinet when Foreign Minister Mutsu Munemitsu resigned to take political responsibility for the Ōtsu Incident, discussed earlier. Meiji at once intervened to promote Enomoto Takeaki as his replacement. This, and other similar imperial interventions which need not be discussed here, alarmed Itō, who felt Meiji was too eager to involve himself directly in contentious political affairs. When Matsukata served notice that he would resign, and as Itō was about to form a new cabinet, Itō told Meiji in 1892: "Henceforth, I want to handle everything myself. Although I shall of course consult Your Majesty's opinion on important matters, I request that all else be entrusted to me."[47] Thus did Itō force Meiji to the political sidelines, much as Meiji's successors would be sidelined by their advisers.

Still, Itō frequently needed Meiji's help in overcoming Diet opposition to his policies as prime minister from August 1892 to September 1896. To illustrate, at Itō's request Meiji issued a rescript in 1893 commanding all government officials, whether civilian or military, to sacrifice one-tenth of their pay for six years to help finance naval construction. Meiji himself

donated 300,000 yen. And in December that year he assisted
Itō with another rescript, ordering the dissolution of the Diet
after the Itō cabinet ran into further troubles with the lower
house. Meiji supported Itō in the same way in June 1894, and
he again helped him when, during Itō's fourth cabinet
(1900–1901), the house of peers threatened to block the proposed budget in protesting a government bill to increase taxes.
Meiji responded with an imperial rescript commanding the
Peers to desist, which they did.

Itō was heavily criticized by the political parties for manipulating Meiji for his own political ends, notwithstanding that
on other occasions the parties themselves manipulated him,
too.[48] Meiji likewise complained that Itō was too overbearing.
In 1891 he said:

> Itō is supremely confident in his talents and very self-
> centered. If anyone else of his calibre could be found,
> the two of them could check and balance each other …
> but no such person is available…. Itō has become an
> overweening egotist, assuming that what Bismarck is
> to Germany … he is to Japan. This makes things very
> difficult. I would like to find an able person who could
> act as a foil to Itō. But I cannot think of one.[49]

Yet while Meiji resented being treated like a puppet, from
his perspective and that of the nation's, the greater problem
was ceaseless conflicts among the *genrō*, which gravely desta-
bilized the government. He was particularly incensed about
this in a conversation with court officials in September 1896,
after Itō had resigned the premiership and it was unclear who

would succeed him (it turned out to be Matsukata). Meiji felt "boundless regret" that the *genrō* could not agree on such matters, especially it was their duty to advise him on appointments. A new cabinet had to reflect the trust of the emperor, but if cabinets were born in contention, the nation would suffer; if his loyal subjects saw disunity among his advisers, they would criticize the government and greater political conflict would ensue.[50] A year later, he stated in the same vein that conflicts between his advisers did not mean that constitutional government should be abandoned, but he felt they made constitutional government a hard system to implement. He said the country sorely needed men like Ōkubo Toshimichi, who had appreciated the importance of unity.[51]

Meiji clearly believed that as an emperor who transcended political conflict it was his duty to foster elite unity based on what was best for the nation as a whole. And in fact, this was Meiji's most significant political contribution, especially in the stormy early years of constitutional government. He continued to play this role later, but with much less urgency, for the crisis of the Sino-Japanese War of 1894–95 united the government and led to an increasing emphasis on compromises with the Diet in the following years. Ironically, as Meiji thus withdrew from intense political involvement behind the scenes in the mid-1890s, his wartime public image as commander-in-chief of the armed forces increasingly reinforced the widespread belief among his subjects that he was a ruling, not just a reigning, god-king, while his ministers of state continued to view him as a constitutional monarch with qualified powers.[52] This gap between public and elite perceptions of the emperor would widen further in later years, particularly during the

reign of Meiji's grandson, Emperor Shōwa. *Technological Advancement*

Meiji and the Rise of the Empire

Throughout his reign Meiji was closely associated in the public mind with the goals of "wealth and power" in Japan's quest for autonomous development. Meiji promoted industrialization by visiting factories, by conferring honors on leading financiers and industrialists, and by officiating at the opening of new bridges and railway lines with great fanfare. When he inaugurated the new Tokyo-Yokohama line in 1872, more than 20,000 people saw him board a special carriage at Shinbashi for the first train journey from Tokyo to Yokohama, where the opening ceremonies were to be held. Upon arriving at the Yokohama station, "His Majesty did not attempt to conceal his satisfaction at the very tasty decorations" of red and white lamps hanging from the station roof and flowers planted on the station grounds.[53]

Meiji appears to have been genuinely interested in new technology. Clara Whitney relates in her diary that on one occasion, in 1878, Meiji looked on as her father "performed several experiments before him in chemistry and physics" and demonstrated how a telegraph and a new burglar alarm worked. Meiji was very pleased, but said, "'I cannot understand. Let the explanation be in Japanese.'"[54] Once, however, Meiji's curiosity backfired. In 1872, while visiting a foundry in Yokohama to observe how molten iron was poured into a mold, the mold suddenly blew up. An officer standing nearby had to shield Meiji from harm as "red hot bits of metal flew all around."[55]

Meiji promoted the development and prestige of the mili-

tary whenever he attended the grand spring and autumn military maneuvers in his capacity as commander-in-chief. These were impressive events, reported extensively by the press. Large crowds would watch as Meiji, splendidly dressed in uniform, traveled with his retinue from the palace to the train station for his journey to the site of the exercises. In April 1890, for instance, the exercises involved the rapid deployment of 50,000 soldiers from Nagoya to Osaka, which they were to defend in cooperation with Japanese battleships off the coast from attack by unnamed enemy forces from across the Pacific, landing at different points along the shoreline.

In the realm of foreign relations Meiji's main public contribution as head of state was to welcome distinguished visitors to Japan, beginning with the visit in 1869 of the Duke of Edinburgh. In 1879 his state guest was Prince Henry of Prussia, and in 1881 he hosted England's Prince George (later King George V) and Prince Albert, both of whom were then serving in the royal navy. Over the years many other foreign dignitaries followed. Meiji performed his ceremonial duties conscientiously. He impressed his English guests in 1881 as "self-possessed and evidently strenuously anxious, though not nervous, to play his part well."[56]

In contrast to his public role, Meiji's specific contributions behind the scenes to Japanese foreign policy-making are harder to pinpoint from available sources. In general, he was regularly consulted by the government, but he did not make foreign policy in his own right any more than he made domestic policy. Yet as a nationalist he entirely shared the pragmatic concern of Japan's leaders with national security, and by formally sanctioning the government's decisions on foreign pol-

icy in his capacity as constitutional monarch, he shared collective responsibility for them. That he felt keenly this sense of responsibility made him cautious when given opportunities to express his own views on specific foreign policy issues. His cautiousness can be illustrated in many episodes of decision-making, but only some of the most important can be discussed here, beginning with the crisis of the Sino-Japanese War.

Essentially, this war was fought over Korea. Korea had been a sensitive issue in Japanese foreign policy since 1873, when Meiji threw his weight behind the government's decision not to invade Korea (then a satellite of China) in response to a perceived Korean insult to Japanese pride. In 1885 Japan had reached an agreement with China, Korea's traditional protector, whereby neither side would commit troops to Korea without first informing the other. However in June 1894—one month before Japan concluded a treaty with Britain which would end many aspects of the "unequal treaties"—Sino-Japanese relations over Korea were badly aggravated by the outbreak of the Tonghak rebellion against the Korean royal court. Without prior notice, China at once sent in troops as requested by the Korean king, and Japan replied by doing likewise. Specifically, on June 6 Meiji was informed that the army would send 3,000 troops to Korea. Seven days later Grand Chamberlain Tokudaiji Sanenori reported to Meiji that the actual number was much higher: 8,000 troops. The army had deceived the emperor concerning its true intentions.[57]

Japan's leaders were manifestly determined not to let China upset the strategic balance of power in Korea and, in the longer run, not to let any Western power gain ascendancy

on the Korean peninsula, which might threaten Japan. This latter concern was prompted by the current "scramble for concessions" by the Western powers in East Asia and more specifically by fears that Russia's construction of the Trans-Siberian Railway (begun in 1891 and completed in 1903) would introduce Russian military power and economic interests into the region. In this volatile context Korea was deemed to be of great strategic importance to Japan. As Yamagata Aritomo expressed this consensus, Japan's military and economic "line of advantage" lay in the Korean peninsula, which was often likened to a "dagger" pointing at the belly of Japan.

Accordingly, in 1894 the Itō cabinet was quite prepared to go to war with China over Korea if necessary. However, Meiji repeatedly asked Itō for an explanation of the escalating crisis with China and insisted upon a diplomatic solution, to the consternation of the army minister. As Itō told the cabinet in July, the emperor "will not easily sanction the opening of hostilities."[58] Meiji indeed delayed his sanction, believing that Japan might not prevail against China's larger forces. Finally, though, government pressure forced him to relent. After he formally ratified the decision at an imperial conference (*gozen kaigi*) attended by the cabinet and high military officials, Japan declared war on China on August 1. Meiji was very distressed by this outcome. He complained to his advisers that although he had sanctioned the decision, it had not been his personal wish to go to war. For this reason he resisted the idea of sending an imperial messenger to report the onset of war to the gods at Ise Shrine, as was customary. But he did make a point of praying at the palace shrine for the welfare of his troops.[59]

Once Japan was at war, with Japanese troops flooding

Korea and north China and the imperial navy also fully engaged, Meiji's concern was to avoid internal rivalries that might impede the war effort. During a speech on August 30, at a ceremony to appoint Yamagata as commander of the army leading the assault, he warned that victory would depend upon "cooperation and close liaison between the civilian and military authorities." He further emphasized that "the respective powers of the imperial headquarters and commanders in the field must be clearly distinguished" and discord between them must be avoided. Furthermore, "field commanders and resident diplomats [in Korea] must take care not to exceed their respective offices. The overall success or failure of the nation does not rest on the battlefield alone."[60] Two weeks later he went by train to Hiroshima, the wartime seat of imperial headquarters and a major point of departure for Japanese units bound for the front. He would not return to Tokyo until May 30, 1895, passing through a hastily-built victory arch on his triumphal procession to the imperial palace.

During the war much was made of Meiji's decisive leadership as commander-in-chief in official pronouncements and in the expanding Japanese press. For instance, it was related that Meiji, always dressed in uniform, diligently followed battle reports and discussed wartime operations with military leaders from early in the morning to late at night. Moreover, it was widely reported that Meiji had generously sent 1,590 casks of *sake* and five million cigarettes to soldiers at the front and that he had donated large sums of money to Yasukuni Shrine, where services for the war dead were continually held.

Resolved to identify himself personally with the trials and tribulations of his officers and men, he subjected himself to

various austerities. In his Hiroshima barracks he lived in a cramped apartment of several sparsely furnished rooms. Instead of a chair, he used a three-legged stool; instead of electric lights, he used candles. He refused the comfort of a warm fire while his troops were freezing in the winter cold overseas.[61] He even ordered that no women should be allowed in his presence. Likening his living quarters to the front, he worked so hard that his attendants were constantly concerned by his deep fatigue.

At the time, Baelz observed that these widely-publicized images of Meiji served to enhance "a quasi-religious worship of the Emperor as the symbolical representative of the nation—a purposeful scattering of ancient seed upon a soil that had now become favorable to its growth. The work of the leading statesmen of Japan has, in this respect, been remarkably successful—perhaps more successful than they hoped or desired."[62] But while Meiji personally identified with the armed forces in seeking to inspire the country to greater patriotic effort, "There is no evidence that the emperor ever originated or influenced a military decision during the war. In fact, the record of his private comments tends only to confirm his irrelevance in such matters."[63] He merely sanctioned the campaigns mapped out by the chiefs of staff. Otherwise his principal wartime function was to symbolize national unity in the emergency of war. It was thus with intense patriotic spirit that the first emergency session of the wartime Diet, which was held in Hiroshima in a hurriedly constructed building which had a canvas roof, unanimously passed the war budget.

Rather than running the war and controlling the military, as the commander-in-chief appeared to be doing, Meiji was

frustrated to see that, notwithstanding his earlier plea for co-operation between imperial headquarters and commanders in the field, the latter sometimes disobeyed orders from Tokyo. In late 1894, for instance, Yamagata moved some of the troops under his command to positions which had not been authorized by Tokyo. Itō subsequently persuaded Meiji to recall Yamagata, although other factors were involved in this decision. But incidents such as this prompted Meiji to complain, in somewhat understated terms, "The army does have a tendency of being difficult to lead."[64] The same problem of military insubordination would later bedevil Emperor Shōwa on a much greater scale.

Towards the end of the war, with victory in sight, Yamagata proposed that Meiji should go to the continent and personally lead the final campaign, if only symbolically. But Meiji's poor health, due to fatigue, precluded this, although the idea was never seriously considered in any event. An imperial prince was sent instead. For his part, Meiji was more determined to end the war through diplomatic negotiations, using England or Russia as an intermediary, and without insisting on territorial gains or an indemnity from China. But it transpired that when China finally capitulated, Japan acquired in the Treaty of Shimonoseki (signed on April 17, 1895) Taiwan and the Pescadores, the Liaotung Peninsula (in south Manchuria), a huge indemnity of 200 million taels, Korea's independence from China, and other significant gains.

A week later, however, in the Triple Intervention, Japan was served with a joint ultimatum by Russia, France, and Germany demanding the return of the Liaotung Peninsula to China. By then Meiji had been moved temporarily to the for-

[handwritten margin note: moved thought he would not allow the govt. Lie?]

[handwritten margin note: wasn't consulted at all?]

mer imperial palace in Kyoto, so that the ambassadors of those countries could not easily reach him to press their case. After having expended his energies following the course of the war, Meiji now seemed at a loss and took to wandering aimlessly in the imperial garden.[65] But he was greatly relieved when the Itō cabinet complied with the ultimatum on May 4. On May 12, he told Sasaki Takayuki, a court adviser, that it had been absolutely necessary to avoid confrontation with these Western powers and that even if Japan had kept the Liaotung Peninsula, it would have cost too much to administer and defend; Japan would have had to divert valuable resources needed to fortify the defenses of Taiwan.[66]

By October 1895 it was clear that Japan's abandonment of the Liaotung Peninsula had only encouraged Russian opportunism. That month, Meiji revealed to Sasaki that he was very worried about Russia's encroachment in Manchuria and northern Korea, through the building of railway lines which China had supported in return for Russian assistance in regaining possession of the Liaotung Peninsula. He regretted that it was not adequately understood in Japan just how aggressive Russia had become.[67] Should, then, Japan ally itself with Britain against the threat posed by Russia? At first Meiji was unsure, and so was the government, when the question of an alliance with Britain arose in 1898.

At an imperial conference in January 1898, by which time Russia had occupied the Liaotung Peninsula and had fortified the naval base at Port Arthur, Itō Hirobumi reviewed Japan's dilemma as follows. If Japan were to ally with Britain in any military confrontation between Britain and Russia in East Asia, this would provoke Japanese hostilities with Russia,

France, and Germany. Hence, Itō opposed an alliance with Britain. But he conceded that if Japan tilted towards Russia, this would isolate Japan from Britain, the strongest naval power in the region. After much debate Meiji approved Yamagata's rather equivocal proposal that for the time being Japan should stay neutral if Britain and Russia went to war.[68]

By 1901 the government of Prime Minister Katsura Tarō, a general from Chōshū and Yamagata's protégé, had decided to pursue the British option in response to diplomatic feelers from London. In December that year Katsura sought Meiji's approval of a draft treaty with Britain. However, Meiji delayed his approval because he wanted the matter brought before a meeting of the *genrō* first. When Yamagata, Matsukata, Ōyama Iwao, and Inoue Kaoru supported Katsura, Meiji still withheld his approval, for he also wanted to ascertain the opinion of Itō Hirobumi, who was then in St. Petersburg. Upon being informed of Katsura's arguments for an alliance with Britain, Itō replied by cable that while in principle he was prepared to go along with Katsura, the alliance should be deferred, to probe Germany's reactions and to avoid damaging Japan's trade with Russia.[69]

Meiji agreed and asked the other *genrō* to reconsider in the light of Itō's opinion. However, Katsura's views ultimately prevailed and the Anglo-Japanese Alliance was concluded, to take effect in January 1902. Its chief purpose was to contain Russia in East Asia and in the process to check France, Russia's ally, in the event of war with Russia. It is somewhat ironic, considering Meiji's hesitation over the Anglo-Japanese Alliance, that when he died the British press published obituaries praising him mainly because of the Alliance. Yet his cau-

tiousness in this instance was consistent with his cautious approach to the decision for war against China in 1894 and his subsequent support for the retrocession of the Liaotung Peninsula. Meiji's essential role was to work for consensus and clarity of purpose in decision-making. As one historian comments, "In general, he was able to hold up decisions while the substance was further studied."[70]

Meiji was also cautious concerning Japan's participation in the Russo-Japanese War of 1904–05. Once again, the strategic significance of Korea figured prominently in Japanese thinking. At an imperial conference attended by senior cabinet members and elder statesmen on June 23, 1903, it was decided that although Japan ultimately wanted a Russian military withdrawal from Manchuria, the most that could be expected in the near future was a settlement in which Japan would recognize Manchuria as a Russian sphere of influence if Russia recognized Korea as a Japanese sphere. At this stage, Meiji personally felt that diplomacy should be given full priority, for the risks of war with Russia, a Western military power, were obvious and despite the apparent consensus of the imperial conference, there were signs of division: Itō Hirobumi and the navy minister were especially reluctant to go to war with Russia.[71]

In the ensuing negotiations, Russia initially appeared cooperative. But by January 1904, it was clear that St. Petersburg was stalling. Therefore, the imperial conference on January 12 decided to warn Russia that peace between Japan and Russia depended upon a quick and favorable Russian response, including above all a willingness to recognize Japan's paramount interests in Korea. However, the Russians remained

noncommittal and on February 3 a meeting of the *genrō* and the Katsura cabinet determined that war with Russia was now inevitable. Knowing that he would be called upon to sanction a war decision on February 4, Meiji, still dressed in his night-clothes, summoned Itō to the palace early that morning and asked him for his opinion. According to one Japanese account, Itō replied that Japan might not be able to defeat Russia, but that by holding the line for a year at the Yalu River, between Manchuria and Korea, Japan could probably persuade the United States to mediate a favorable peace; Itō then recommended war.[72]

Whether Itō indeed said this cannot be confirmed, but Meiji apparently concluded that war had to be waged, whatever the risks. At an imperial conference later that day, with the elder statesmen and key members of the cabinet present, he sanctioned the government's war decision.[73] On February 8 Japan opened hostilities with a surprise attack on Port Arthur; war on Russia was not formally declared until February 10.

This time Meiji followed the conflict from the imperial palace in Tokyo, where imperial headquarters was now located. As in the Sino-Japanese War he received daily briefings on the fighting, but also as before, he himself did not participate in making battle decisions. And again, the popular idea that he was in control of Japanese forces was contradicted by reality.

An instance of this occurred at one point in the autumn of 1904. The Third Army, under the command of the Manchurian army general headquarters, unilaterally disobeyed orders to attack north and instead attacked south, towards Port Arthur. When he learned of this, Meiji was very upset that imperial

headquarters could not enforce discipline through the chain of command. He therefore instructed Grand Chamberlain Tokudaiji to have Prime Minister Katsura report to him on the matter immediately. Katsura delayed, however, in order to find out more about what had happened at the front, and by the time he audienced with Meiji it was too late to halt the Third Army. Meiji bitterly accepted this fait accompli but was angry that Japanese journalists had published the fact that orders had been disobeyed. He warned Katsura that this could weaken the army's faith in his authority, to the detriment of the war effort.[74] Exactly the same dilemma, of how to exert central control over armies in the field, would preoccupy Emperor Hirohito during the Manchurian Incident and thereafter in the 1930s.

During the Russo-Japanese War Meiji again sent gifts to the front and donated funds to various wartime causes in Japan. He and the Empress strongly supported the Japanese Red Cross (formed in 1886), which assisted the army in caring for 70,000 Russian prisoners of war in Japan; much was made in government propaganda of this display of imperial benevolence.[75] As for his personal wartime routine, it was much less austere than earlier at Hiroshima, mainly because he now suffered from diabetes, a fact which was not revealed to his subjects. Sequestered in the palace, he spent much of his time writing poetry; 7,526 of the 90,000 poems that he produced during his entire lifetime dated from this period. Their predominant theme was his sympathy for the suffering of the troops.

Japanese losses were indeed immense. Before troops under the command of General Nogi Maresuke finally seized Port

Arthur in January 1905, Japan had sustained more than 50,000 casualties in that campaign. Mukden, in Manchuria, was taken in March at the cost of 16,553 Japanese deaths with another 53,475 Japanese wounded (Russian losses there included 8,705 dead and 51,388 wounded). Altogether, nearly 90,000 Japanese lives were lost in the Russo-Japanese War. Only after Admiral Tōgō Heihachirō's ships sank Russia's Baltic Fleet in the well-known Battle of Tsushima Straits, which was fought in May, did Russia and Japan eventually agree on peace talks mediated by the American president Theodore Roosevelt.

The result was the Treaty of Portsmouth, concluded in September 1905, which gave Japan the Russian leases in Manchuria and control of the South Manchurian Railway, as well as the southern half of Sakhalin Island. Russia, moreover, at last agreed to withdraw its troops from Manchuria and to recognize Japan's paramount interests in Korea. However, Japan did not receive the indemnity the people expected after so many deaths. This, and other grievances, led to massive protests across the country and especially in Tokyo's Hibiya Park, where violent clashes between angry crowds and the police resulted in seventeen recorded deaths and over 1,000 wounded. From the palace nearby Meiji heard the sound of guns fired by the police to clear the Park. Appalled, he exclaimed, "The military police have fired on the people!"[76] Nevertheless, in October Meiji sanctioned the Treaty as the Katsura government advised him to do.

Japan's unprecedented victory over Russia captured headlines around the world. In some quarters, such as among the socialists in England, Japan was now hailed as a liberator of oppressed peoples from the yoke of Western colonial rule; in

others, Japan was regarded as a dangerous "yellow peril." But Britain's response in 1905 was to renew and revise the Anglo-Japanese Alliance, with the result that now Japan recognized British interests in India while Britain recognized Japan's interests in Korea. This latter provision freed Japan to negotiate the establishment of a protectorate in Korea, which made Japan responsible for Korean foreign relations. It also anticipated the willingness of Britain, and the other Western powers for that matter, to accept Japan's annexation of Korea in 1910.

After the Russo-Japanese War, Yamagata argued for a strong interventionist policy to safeguard Japan's strategic interests in Korea, whereas Itō generally favored a softer line, emphasizing Japan's general guidance of Korea, particularly in the area of economic and cultural relations. Since Meiji shared Itō's approach, he was pleased to appoint him Resident-General in Korea in 1905. The Korean ruler, Emperor Kojong, however, who had unsuccessfully opposed the establishment of the protectorate, proved troublesome and was forced to abdicate in July 1907. His successor, Sunjong, was much more cooperative. Nevertheless, there were growing signs of violent anti-Japanese resistance throughout Korea, and in this setting, by 1909 Prime Minister Katsura, Yamagata Aritomo, and the military leadership as a whole advocated annexation to achieve full political and economic control of Korea.[77]

The historian Suyama Yukio has discovered evidence that Meiji adamantly opposed annexation, although Meiji's specific reasons are unknown.[78] Perhaps Itō influenced Meiji's thinking in this regard. Itō, who resigned as resident-general in

June 1909, now admitted that annexation was a strong possibility given the problem of Korean resistance, but he had always felt that annexation could also make it harder to manage the peninsula. On a more personal level, for many years Meiji had stressed good relations between the imperial house and the Korean court, and to that end in 1907 he had sent his heir, Yoshihito, to Korea (see next chapter) to strengthen ties with Sunjong. Similarly in 1908 Meiji had welcomed Sunjong's heir, the new Korean crown prince, to Japan for a period of study.

Consequently, in many discussions with Katsura and other government officials Meiji refused to agree to annexing Korea. But Itō's sudden assassination by a Korean nationalist on October 26, 1909—which, in view of their long-standing cooperation, understandably caused Meiji much sorrow—left him without a major ally on the annexation question. For a time Meiji still held out, and on one occasion, when Yamagata referred to the Korean Yi Wan-yong, who had persuaded the Korean court to accept annexation, Meiji burst out with the comment that Yi was a "monstrous person" who had punished his political opponents "with great cruelty."[79] Yet once the *genrō* and the cabinet decided upon annexation, Meiji felt he had no choice as a constitutional monarch but to sanction the decision with the imperial will on August 22, 1910.[80] That same day in Seoul, the Korean government signed a treaty of annexation by which Emperor Sunjong abdicated his sovereignty to the Japanese throne; on August 29, Meiji promulgated an Edict of Annexation. Korea would remain under Japanese control until the end of World War II.

The annexation of Korea completed the imperial legacy of the Meiji era. But there is another aspect of this legacy which

cannot be ignored. It concerns Emperor Meiji and the problem of civilian control of the military in the course of empire
building.

As we have seen, Meiji was well aware of the implications
for his authority of occasional breakdowns in the military
chain of command during both the Sino-Japanese and Russo-
Japanese conflicts. He seems to have been generally indifferent, however, to the growing political independence of the
military from civilian control. In large measure, this was probably due to Yamagata's influence over Meiji, which was as
great in military affairs as Itō's was in political affairs. In 1893
Meiji said to Yamagata: "As you are a general on active duty
... on all important military matters I will seek your advice, so
please reply candidly."[81]

In fact, Meiji had long relied upon Yamagata's advice concerning military issues. He had agreed when Yamagata peti-
tioned him in 1881 to the effect that rescripts concerning the
armed services need not require the prime minister's authority
since the emperor was supreme commander of the armed
forces. Accordingly, in January the next year Meiji duly issued
the Rescript to Soldiers and Sailors, which, drafted by Yamagata, emphasized the importance of loyalty, valor, and moral
rectitude. A key passage also reads, "neither be led astray by
current opinions nor meddle in politics, but with single heart
fulfil your essential duty...." While this ostensibly implies a
desire to prevent the military from interfering in politics, Yamagata's real motive was to protect the military from outside
political interference.

Furthermore, "The extension of this principle of isolating
the military from politics is found in the regulation Yamagata

originated in May 1900 which required the service ministers in the cabinet to be regular officers of the highest rank."[82] That is, Yamagata persuaded Meiji to issue an imperial ordinance that year which changed the service regulations so that henceforth only generals and lieutenant-generals on active duty would be eligible for appointment as army minister in the cabinet; similarly, only admirals and vice-admirals on active duty could serve as navy minister. Yamagata's goal was to ensure that the army and navy, and not party politicians, would always have the decisive say in filling these posts. Again, Meiji seems not to have anticipated the long-range consequence, which was to enable the armed services to fell a cabinet they opposed simply by withdrawing a service minister. This "tripwire" gave the military enormous leverage over the cabinet. It was removed in 1913 but reinstated in 1936.

During the Meiji period the elder statesmen collectively mediated between the emperor and the military and thereby prevented the political autonomy of the military from becoming the sort of major problem in foreign policy-making which subsequently characterized the early Shōwa period. But by deferring to Yamagata in military matters, Meiji, unwittingly perhaps, significantly helped to sow the seeds of this problem.

Meiji's Last Years

The acquisition of empire greatly increased Meiji's international stature as the monarch of a rising power in Asia. He was particularly gratified that in 1906 Prince Arthur of Connaught visited Japan to invest him with the Knight of the Garter at a special palace ceremony on February 20. After Prince Arthur buckled "the Garter below the Emperor's knee," a band played "God Save the King." Algernon Mitford, who was on hand, adds, "The effect was electric, and lent a charm to the whole ceremony."[83] Meiji later reciprocated by pinning the ribbon and star of the Order of the Chrysanthemum on Arthur's tunic.

Yet, Meiji's last years were troubled, both by politics and by poor health. Politically, Japan had entered a new phase in which power alternated between the cabinets of Prime Ministers Katsura Tarō (1901–1906, 1908–1911) and Prince Saionji Kinmochi (1906–1908, 1911–1912), Meiji's friend from childhood who had succeeded Itō as president of the Seiyūkai in 1903. Whereas Katsura mostly represented the interests of his patron, Yamagata, and the ideal of bureaucratic, non-party cabinets, Saionji, despite his aristocratic lineage, spoke for the interests of the party movement.

Having built up a strong personal faction in the military, the civil service, and the house of peers, Yamagata sought to isolate Itō, his old rival, from the Seiyūkai, and used Meiji to this end. In 1903 he pressed Meiji for an imperial rescript commanding Itō, who had attacked Prime Minister Katsura's ambitious agenda for naval expansion, to give up the presidency of the Seiyūkai and accept appointment as president of the privy council, where he would be cut off from party politics. It was only with much reluctance that Meiji complied with Yamagata's request, for he profoundly disliked being manipulated by Yamagata in this way.[84] Meiji was no less dismayed when, without keeping him fully informed, Yamagata maneuvered in July 1908 to promote Katsura Tarō as the next prime minister after the resignation of the first Saionji cabinet. Meiji suspected that Yamagata had intrigued to undermine

[handwritten margin note: didn't like being manipulated but then it's ok to be.]

Saionji, so that Katsura could return to power.[85] But Meiji found it impossible to check Yamagata, who marginalized him politically, just as he would marginalize Emperor Taishō.

Another quite different problem arose during the last years of Meiji's reign, in the form of a small but vociferous socialist movement which was highly critical of the monarchy and indeed the entire political and economic order. Centered especially on the Heiminsha, or Commoner's Society, in Tokyo, most of the socialists energetically opposed the Russo-Japanese War for cruelly sacrificing the lives of countless conscripted soldiers to benefit the rich and powerful in Japan. The following verse from Yosano Akiko's familiar poem, "Do Not Offer Your Life," which she wrote for her brother in the army, typified this anti-war mood:

Do not offer your life.
The Emperor himself does not go
To battle.
The Imperial Heart is deep;
How could he ever wish
That men shed their blood,
That men die like beasts,
That man's glory be in death?

Using police legislation enacted in 1900, the state easily contained this socialist movement. But in June 1908 there were clashes in the streets between the police and a handful of self-styled anarchists, including followers of Kōtoku Shūsui (Denjirō), the leading Japanese anarchist of the period. As they were arrested they shouted radical slogans and carried red flags emblazoned with the words, "anarchism" and "anarchist communism." Such was the reaction in establishment circles that this so-called "Red Flag Incident" contributed to the fall of the fairly liberal Saionji cabinet that year.

The actual threat of anarchism to the imperial state and capitalist order was insignificant, but to Japan's ruling elites it seemed real enough. Hence in January 1911 Kōtoku and eleven other anarchists were convicted and executed for having allegedly conspired to assassinate Emperor Meiji in the "High Treason Incident." Before these executions took place Meiji asked Katsura whether the death sentences should not be reduced to life imprisonment, through a special imperial pardon. Katsura refused; he wanted no clemency for enemies of the state. But he did approve of a huge imperial grant for medical aid to the poor, hoping that private philanthropy would follow suit in dealing with the social origins of political radicalism. Meanwhile, the authorities increased their vigilance toward suspected radicals, and patriotic organizations such as the Imperial Reservists' Association (Teikoku zaigō gunjinkai), which had been formed in 1910 by General Tanaka Giichi and other officers loyal to Yamagata, publicly pledged their patriotic readiness to defend the emperor and the imperial institution from the menace of left-wing revolution.

Apart from these unsettling political developments, Meiji's later years were marred by the worsening of his diabetes and by Bright's Disease (an ailment affecting the kidneys). On many state occasions, he struck observers as being deeply fatigued. Still, prior to the summer of 1912, there was no indication that Meiji would die that year at the relatively young age of sixty. In January 1912 he attended the annual New Year's poetry party at the palace, as usual. He fell ill in February but soon recovered and was able to maintain his usual schedule of appointments. On May 30, for instance, he attended the graduation ceremony of the Army Middle Preparatory School, where he reviewed the graduating class and gave out prizes. On June 28 he welcomed the former president of Harvard University, Charles William Eliot, in the company of various Japanese and American dignitaries.

On July 10, however, when he visited Tokyo Imperial University to give out prizes at the graduation ceremony, he complained of a "washed-out feeling" and had trouble climbing the stairs. Five days later, at a meeting of the privy council, Meiji fell asleep in his chair after trembling badly, his face strained, as he took his seat.[86] On July 19 he was back at his desk, but was too weary to work, and when he stood up he staggered and fell. Medical specialists from Tokyo Imperial University were summoned to assist the court doctors in his treatment. The Empress, the elder statesmen, Prime Minister Saionji and his cabinet, the privy council, and high military officials were all informed that Meiji was seriously ill. The government also decided to inform the public at once.

Over the following days the newspapers carried detailed reports on his weakening pulse rate and the decline of his other bodily functions. Prayers were offered for his recovery and "Very large numbers gathered in the neighborhood of the palace, many of them kneeling or prostrate on the ground. There was a curious hush in the air...."[87] Finally, Meiji died of heart failure, at forty-three minutes past midnight on July 30. The nation was swept with a profound sense of loss. The novelist Tokutomi Roka wrote, "The emperor's death has closed the book of Meiji history.... I felt as if my own life had been broken off."[88] Yamagata, too, was moved to say in a poem,

The heavenly light
has today gone out
leaving the world
in darkness.

Yamagata later had a shrine built on his property at Odawara and often prayed there, pledging always to honor the spirit of the departed emperor.[89]

Meiji's funeral procession took place in Tokyo on the night of September 13. Dense crowds of people stood quietly by as a team of oxen pulled a wagon bearing Meiji's casket; "The only sound" was "the soft crunching of the wheels of the wagon on the sand, and the creaking of the axles."[90] After the procession reached a special hall that had been built on the Aoyama parade grounds, his successor, Emperor Taishō, Prime Minister Saionji, and Imperial Household Minister Watanabe Chiaki, gave short speeches eulogizing Meiji. His casket was then transported by train to Kyoto where his remains were interred on September 15 in the Momoyama Imperial Mausoleum located in the Fushimi section of the city. The only discordant note in this period of national mourning was the news that one of the great heroes of the Russo-Japanese War, General Nogi, and his wife had committed ritual suicide at their home on September 13. To many Japanese, Nogi's death evoked nostalgia for the medieval samurai tradition of loyally following one's lord in death. Others, however, thought that Nogi's gesture was anachronistic and at odds with the spirit of modernity which Meiji had symbolized.

As the first emperor to make public appearances and to have his photograph taken, Meiji was a man of commanding presence. In its obituary *The Standard* emphasized to British readers that although he had walked with a slight limp (perhaps due to rheumatism), "his height—five feet, seven inches — made him conspicuous among a people not generally running to great stature. His eyebrows, heavy and black, had the exact slant to be seen in antique manly beauty." *The Westminster Gazette* similarly observed that in public Meiji had projected "a calm, dignified composure."[91] Altogether, Meiji's dignified demeanor and forceful personality made him the only modern Japanese emperor who can be called charismatic.

Yet if Meiji looked the part of emperor, he did not rule Japan in the direct sense often attributed to him by contemporary writers. Instead, he is significant because he decisively defined for his successors, Taishō and Shōwa, the role of a modern constitutional monarch in the Meiji constitutional context. The well-known contemporary journalist Tokutomi Sohō, who regarded Meiji as a model in this respect, admired him because he "never deserted his Ministers"; he "always welcomed suggestions from the Elder Statesmen and Ministers" and "never signed a law or ordinance without ascertaining for himself whether it was desirable. He was a painstaking, studious, monarch...."[92]

Meiji took his duties seriously because he took himself very seriously. Just as he never completely lost the shyness which Mitford and later Baelz discerned in him (notwithstanding his exterior confidence), Meiji always retained the fiery, impatient temperament that he had exhibited in childhood whenever other people crossed him. A strong-willed man, he expected at first that he would rule, not just reign. But when constitutional limits were imposed upon his powers, this same demand to be taken seriously drove him to carve out a significant political role in consulting, encouraging, and warning his ministers, rather like the English monarch in Walter Bagehot's familiar characterization.

This manner of exerting informal imperial influence was in fact neccessary in an oligarchical system of rule where the elder statesmen and other political leaders invariably turned to the emperor to referee their own conflicts. Japan's elites often used Meiji to their own ends, but equally they accepted his arbitration even when it went against them and listened to, and respected, his views. This enabled Meiji to hold the government together in times of crisis, and it enabled him to participate as a member of the ruling elite in governing the country. In the informal process of "working through the court" to achieve consensus on policy, he performed the essential role of legitimating government decisions by ratifying them with the imperial will. This legitimating function of the throne was especially imperative when government policies risked the fate of the nation, as in the decisions for war in 1894 and 1904.

Any balanced assessment of Meiji must acknowledge the negative aspects of his reign, too. Japan's victorious wars brought glory to Meiji, as well as to the nation, but only at great human cost on the battlefield. Success in war and diplomacy also masked a problem to which Meiji turned a blind eye: the growing political independence of the military from civilian control. Politically, in his last years, the crystallization of a socialist movement indicated that there were Japanese for whom national wealth and power meant exploitation and injustice. That the imperial institution was closely linked with the systematic repression of radical dissent, as in the High Treason Incident, may not have been directly attributable to Meiji himself, but it showed that "imperial benevolence" was conditional on absolute loyalty to the state.

Finally, Meiji symbolized the rise of modern Japan, and it is quite true that, by the time he died, he was widely "associated, at a noble distance, with constitutionalism, much more closely with education, inextricably with victory in war and international prestige, generously with benevolence in small cash grants and large outpourings of concern, personally with culture in the form of poetry and patronage, and always with the achievement of civilization."[93] Yet, the emperor cult in which these and other images predominated was streaked with an irrational devotion to Meiji that persisted long after his death. In 1913 the Diet resolved to build a large shrine in his honor, in the Yoyogi area of Tokyo. Before Meiji Shrine was completed in 1920, thousands of young people volunteered to help build the Shrine and to plant trees from all parts of Japan in the spacious surrounding parkland. Such was their fanatical veneration of Meiji that some young women reportedly wished to be buried alive under the Shrine. Fortunately, they were persuaded to offer locks of hair instead.[94]

Cult
of
the emperor

TAISHŌ
(YOSHIHITO)

•

The "Retired" Emperor

Emperor Taishō early in his reign.

So little has been written about Taishō in Japanese, and even less in English, that he is seldom remembered today. When he is mentioned, it is usually in very unflattering terms. One author states, "Devoid of any qualities describable as refined," as crown prince "he turned dandiness into laughable, then pitiable, foppishness." He so wanted to imitate Kaiser Wilhelm of Germany that he "adopted the Wilhelmine waxed-handlebar mustache, which looked as idiotic on the Japanese prince as it did on William."[1]

In many respects, Taishō was indeed an eccentric figure. Yet there is more to his story than that. It is well to bear in mind that at the beginning of his reign, Taishō was viewed very favorably by his subjects. The charisma of his office and the fact that he was Meiji's son and heir contributed to his positive public image. In addition, not that many years had passed since the people of Tokyo had celebrated his marriage on May 10, 1900. Yoshihito, then aged twenty-one, had married Sadako, the fourth daughter of Prince Kujō Michitaka, who was then only sixteen herself. "The whole city was in gala dress" that sunny day. Great crowds lined the street as the young couple "drove away in a fine coach" to the crown prince's palace in Aoyama after their private wedding ceremony at the imperial palace shrine.[2] When the crown princess gave birth to their first son, the future Shōwa Emperor, Michi-no-miya Hirohito, on April 29, 1901, this event too stirred public interest in the crown prince and his family. In 1902 a second son, Chichibu-no-miya Yasuhito Shinnō, was born. There followed the birth of two more sons, Takamatsu-no-miya Nobuhito in 1905 and Mikasa-no-miya in 1915.

Yoshihito's extensive tours, which were particularly news-worthy given that Meiji now rarely left the palace, had also made the crown prince a familiar public figure. His tour to Tohoku in 1902 was his first main expedition. Over the next five years he visited the Kansai area (1903), Ise (November 1905), the Kure naval base (December 1905), and the Unzen region of Kyushu (May 1907). Then in October 1907 he represented Meiji on a state visit to Korea, the first trip overseas by a Japanese crown prince. This goodwill tour understandably received much publicity in Japan.

Accompanied on the cruiser *Kajima* by Admiral Tōgō Heihachirō, Prince Arisugawa Taruhito, General Katsura Tarō, and other dignitaries, Yoshihito arrived at Inchon on October 16, where he was met by the Korean crown prince. He then went by train to Seoul, the Korean capital, and was taken in a horse-drawn carriage to his lodgings at the headquarters of the Japanese Resident-General Itō Hirobumi. The next day Yoshihito was received by Emperor Sunjong, upon whom he conferred the badge and necklace of the Grand Order of Merit on behalf of Emperor Meiji. On October 18 he inspected Japanese troops stationed in Seoul and met with

Japanese officials in the evening. After another day of meetings at the Korean court Yoshihito departed Korea via Inchon on October 20.[3] In November, Meiji ordered that a special commemorative medal be struck to honor what was widely regarded as a successful Korean tour during which Yoshihito had acquitted himself well.

There followed further tours within Japan, beginning with Kyushu as soon as Yoshihito returned from Korea; Yamaguchi and Tokushima Prefectures (April 1908); Tohoku (September 1908); Gifu and Kyoto (1910); and Hokkaido (August 1911).[4] By 1912, he had visited most parts of the country.

Consequently, after he succeeded Meiji on the throne the newspapers were already predisposed to cover Taishō's every public appearance, thereby reflecting, and also stimulating, greater popular interest in him. This attention was evident when, together with his chief-aide-de-camp, the grand chamberlain, and the imperial household minister, he visited the Taishō Exposition on June 18, 1914. Upon arrival at the main hall in a horse-drawn carriage, he was greeted by Prime Minister Ōkuma Shigenobu and other officials. He then went inside to inspect the various displays, which included porcelains from different regions of Japan in the Crafts Hall; diverse techniques of extracting oil and ore in the Mining Hall; food products and artifacts from Korea, Taiwan, and Manchuria in the Empire Hall, and so forth. Along the way he bought candy at a stall and frequently paused for explanations of the exhibits, to which he typically responded, "*ah sō desu ka*" ("is that so?"), much as his son, Hirohito, would awkwardly do when touring Japan during the Occupation many years later.[5] Taishō's visit did much to advertise the Exposition, which was held to promote industry, and seven million tickets were sold.

That Emperor Taishō was quite popular in these early years is likewise apparent in the nationwide celebrations that marked the completion of his enthronement ceremonies, held in Kyoto in November 1915. On November 11 the *Osaka Mainichi* reported in detail how, at a prepublicized time, Prime Minister Ōkuma led the nation in a "banzai" cheer for Taishō while warships at sea fired the first of one hundred salutes. All across Japan that day there were large parades in which the participants carried rising sun flags and portable shrines (*mikoshi*) through the streets, and at nightfall, lanterns.[6] Theaters and cinemas were closed for the occasion, as were businesses, shops, and department stores like Mitsukoshi on the Ginza in Tokyo, after doing a brisk business selling souvenirs imprinted with the chrysanthemum, the symbol of the imperial house. This commercialization of the monarchy, which had begun in the late Meiji period, would gain even more momentum later in Taishō's reign.

While Taishō was generally honored by his subjects, he was regarded from the beginning of his reign with no little skepticism by people who were closer to him and who knew him well. Empress Shōken, for one, was worried about his "political inexperience." Within a month of Meiji's death she expressly asked Prince Saionji Kinmochi to assist Taishō in the performance of his duties.[7] Yamagata Aritomo similarly arranged for Katsura's concurrent appointment as lord keeper of the privy seal and grand chamberlain so that Katsura could guide Taishō and, one may guess, so that Yamagata himself could more easily influence Taishō through Katsura. Katsura served in this dual capacity at court from August 12 to December 21, 1912, when, at Yamagata's prodding, Taishō appointed him to succeed Saionji as prime minister.

Taishō was doubtless a political novice, but his so-called "political inexperience" may well have been a coded reference to some greater deficiency that others perceived in him. Asked to report his initial impressions of Taishō, the British Ambassador Sir Claude MacDonald, who had thought very highly of Meiji, informed London after their first meeting in September 1912: "Intellectually [the Taishō Emperor] is generally supposed to be somewhat wanting and that is certainly the opinion the casual observer would arrive at after several moments' conversation."[8] Thus, when he took office, the 123rd emperor of Japan was seen as a problem by many people who dealt with him directly. To understand more clearly why this was so requires a look at his earlier life.

Crown Prince Yoshihito

Within three weeks of his birth at the Aoyama palace, on the morning of August 30, 1879, Prince Haru-no-miya, as Yoshihito was first known, was diagnosed as suffering from meningitis. Despite the severity of this illness, he soon recovered and in 1880 was entrusted to the care of Prince Nakayama Tadayasu, in whose house he lived until he was seven, when he moved back to the Aoyama palace. In 1901 Dr. Baelz observed: "As a relic of the meningitis from which he suffered in early childhood, the Crown Prince is morbidly restless and lacks the power of concentration. These disorders have now assumed the form of a craving for travel," especially to the imperial villas at Hayama and Numazu, which Yoshihito visited whenever he could over the years.[9] He was also prone to fitful bursts of temper, and in this nervous irritability he resembled his father.

Both as a child and an adult Yoshihito suffered from repeated attacks of the common cold, pneumonia, and influenza. Inevitably, his chronic ill health caused Meiji great anxiety. In November 1884, for instance, when Meiji was informed that Yoshihito had a bad case of influenza, he urgently ordered that he be given regular reports on the boy's medical treatment and instructed Prince Nakayama to pray for Yoshihito's recovery. Then, when Yoshihito again fell ill in May 1885, and his doctors disagreed over the merits of treating him with Chinese or Western medicine, Meiji pointedly intervened to ensure that henceforth only Western medicine would be used. That Yoshihito was not formally designated crown prince until 1887 was due to Meiji's constant concern about his health.

It appears that Meiji was not always told the truth about Yoshihito's condition. In February 1900 Baelz agreed with the Japanese court physicians that Yoshihito was fit enough to get married in May. But they also agreed not to tell Meiji that Yoshihito was underweight due to a recent illness, since Meiji had stipulated that the marriage should not take place "until the body weight had been fully recovered," as Baelz writes. In this deception they were encouraged by Itō Hirobumi and Prince Arisugawa, who were determined to have Yoshihito marry as soon as possible. Their reason: they thought it would be improper for Yoshihito "to touch any other woman before his marriage."[10] Clearly, Yoshihito had strong sexual urges which were no less remarkable than his father's, and which were scarcely diminished by his chronic ill-health. Nor did marrying Sadako prevent his womanizing; far from it.

Meiji's almost obsessive concern for the physical well-being of the future emperor may explain why Yoshihito's attendants were instructed to throw him from the boat into the sea at Hayama, on the shore of Sagami Bay south of Tokyo, to develop his stamina. So, too, were his companions encouraged to drag Yoshihito under the waves to make him swim harder. In this same Spartan spirit Yoshihito did his best to strengthen himself physically, by going on long walks along the beach and into the countryside near Hayama. Perhaps in sympathy with his father's patriotic austerities during the Sino-Japanese War, he took cold baths regularly, did rigorous calisthenics, and often went horseback riding—for which his passion matched Meiji's—again to build up his strength.

But Yoshihito never shook off his vulnerability to illness and his reputation for physical frailty. After his Korean tour the government debated whether he should go on a goodwill tour to the United States, as the American government had proposed, and thence to Europe. Baelz, who had returned to Europe, was invited back to Japan in late 1907 to give his opinion. Ultimately, he vetoed the idea after concluding that Yoshihito was not physically strong enough for so strenuous a tour.[11] Yoshihito was indeed frail: in May 1913 the newspapers reported with great concern the fact that he had succumbed to an attack of pneumonia so soon after taking office. Emperor Taishō's recurring bouts of illness would be front-page news for many years.

Meiji personally kept track of Yoshihito's physical progress when he saw the crown prince once a week, on Saturdays, at the imperial palace. Kanroji Osanaga, one of Yoshihito's close friends, remembers, "The Crown Prince would bow low before the Emperor who, though nodding encouragement, would remain silent throughout the audience." But if Yoshihito's arrow hit the mark in a session of archery, Meiji would exclaim, "Excellent!," the only word Kanroji ever heard him speak on these occasions.[12]

"Excellent" was definitely not a word Meiji would have used regarding Yoshihito's intellectual achievements. Here it must be emphasized that there is nothing in the diary of Dr. Baelz, who examined Yoshihito routinely, or in the available Japanese primary sources, to suggest that he was mentally ill before he became emperor. Indeed, it is doubtful that he was ever mentally ill in the generally accepted senses of the term. Rather, if in 1912 MacDonald found him intellectually "wanting," it was probably because Yoshihito was just not very bright. Even the authorized history of his reign admits that as a child he had unusual difficulty learning how to read and write *kanji* (characters).[13]

Meiji and his advisers repeatedly debated the problem of Yoshihito's poor educational progress. Noting that Yoshihito did not like to study, Itō (in his capacity as imperial household minister) and Minister of Education Mori Arinori recommended in April 1886 that a new set of textbooks be prepared for Yoshihito. Meiji agreed, and also commanded Motoda Eifu and Nishimura Shigeki to assist Yumoto Takehiko, who had been put in charge of Yoshihito's education, in finding ways to make him work harder at his studies.

Thus far, Yoshihito had been tutored with selected classmates at a special school, the Tōgū-gogakumonsho, which had been established for him at the Aoyama detached palace.

But in September 1887 it was decided to send him to the Peers' School, where it was hoped a more disciplined and competitive atmosphere would bring out the best in him. Unfortunately, he missed many weeks due to illness and fell a year behind in his studies. He finally graduated from the elementary to the middle school course in 1893, but in 1894 he returned to the Tōgū-gogakumonsho, which had been relocated to the Akasaka detached palace where he now lived. There, he was tutored in the Chinese classics, Japanese literature and history, world history and politics, economics, French, and other subjects. By then his ability to write *kanji* had improved, and like his father he enjoyed composing *waka*. This interest continued into later years; in 1914, Taishō said that he found that writing poetry provided a valuable respite from the heavy responsibilities and pressures of his office.[14] Bōjō Toshinaga, who attended and otherwise admired Taishō, concedes, however, that his poems were generally undistinguished.[15]

One's overall impression, then, is that Yoshihito was "intellectually challenged," as we might say today. Some of Taishō's sympathizers, including Princess Nashimoto Itsuko, state that he had a "surprisingly good memory" for names and faces. But that he typically found it necessary, when emperor, to ask many of his visitors to give him their photographs for future reference, implies that his memory was not so good after all.[16] However, to suggest that Yoshihito was not very bright is not to imply that he was entirely lacking in imagination. For example, when he and friends were spending a few days in 1890 at the Hakone detached palace, he formed a "ghost story society." The group met in a bath-house illuminated only with a small paper lantern which cast ominous shadows on the wall as the members told harrowing stories to frighten each other. Also, he evidently had an inquisitive nature. Takahashi Korekiyo, who served as prime minister from November 1921 to June 1922, relates that when he was a bureau chief in the ministry of agriculture and commerce early in his career, Yoshihito, then aged seven or eight, constantly pestered him with questions about animals when they visited the Agricultural and Forestry School in Komaba.[17]

Unfortunately, though, Yoshihito's inquisitiveness was not encouraged. Takekoshi Yosaburō once recalled that in 1899 Minister of Communications Yoshikawa Akimasa was troubled by his inability to answer Yoshihito's detailed questions on a certain technical matter. When informed of this, Itō Hirobumi asked Yoshihito, "I hear that Your Majesty has asked Yoshikawa various questions, but is this necessary?" According to Takekoshi, the crown prince replied, "No, it isn't necessary. They were only questions that came to me on impulse." Itō then said, "Because ministers have the confidence of the Emperor, if it is not really necessary for Your Majesty [to ask questions], it probably would be best if you did not do so in so much detail."[18]

Considerations of court protocol and etiquette likewise constrained Yoshihito from taking initatives. As Itō himself told Baelz in 1900, "It is really very hard to be born a crown prince. Directly he comes into the world he is swaddled in etiquette, and when he gets a little bigger he has to dance to the fiddling of his tutors and advisers." Itō, Baelz reports, then "made a movement with his fingers as if he were pulling the strings of a marionette."[19]

Not surprisingly, Yoshihito turned to his family for personal distractions from this kind of pressure. Much more a family man than Meiji, he seemed happiest when playing with his children. Baelz frequently recalls that Yoshihito always took great pride in showing the boys to him: "His paternal delight in these little ones is most touching."[20] But the constraints of life at court grew even tighter once Yoshihito became emperor. Hirohito later said of Taishō, "When he was the Crown Prince he was very cheerful and lively.... After he ascended the throne everything became very rigid and restricted. He was weak physically, so he finally became ill."[21]

From an early age Yoshihito exhibited certain egalitarian tendencies which might well have reflected both a personal revolt against the emphasis at court on status and a reaction on his part to being manipulated like a marionette. When his family stayed at one of the imperial villas by the sea, as a boy Yoshihito often dismayed his attendants by wandering off by himself to visit a local family who lived in a nearby farmhouse. There he would relax and enjoy tea and cakes served by his hosts.[22] In later years at Hayama and Numazu, he would stroll the beach and talk casually with fishermen. He often bought their whole catch of sea bream.

As a young man Yoshihito also liked to visit, unannounced, the barracks of the Konoe Regiment, to which he was attached for the purposes of his military education, to eat and drink with the officers and men. Of the rather plain fare he reportedly once said, "This food is good enough for soldiers and I, too, am a soldier." Once, in 1896, Yoshihito appeared at an officers' club, carrying his own silver cup and in excellent humor. He exclaimed to everyone present, "Who doesn't like *sake*? Let's have some *sake*!"[23] Had he been able to do so, he probably would have chosen the life of an officer, with its more natural comradeship, rather than the life of a crown prince or emperor.

Far preferring informality to stiff protocol, Yoshihito perhaps unconsciously used the pastime of smoking with his guests to put them at ease. He himself was a chain-smoker, and both before and after he became emperor he would offer cigarettes to any and all visitors, whether they were smokers or not. The Seiyūkai politician Hara Kei (Takashi) recalled that in 1913, he had occasion to accompany Taishō in the imperial train on a journey from Kyoto to Shizuoka. Taishō instructed a servant to pass around cigarettes and invited Hara and the others present to smoke at their leisure. Taishō boasted that he had been drinking and smoking from an early age but conceded that he should try and cut down his smoking to ten cigarettes a day.[24] He was also very fond of pipes. He once presented a French Meerschaum pipe as a gift to one of his teachers, Motoori Toyokai (the great grandson of the famous Tokugawa thinker Motoori Norinaga). Lighting a similar pipe of his own, he said "From now on let's compete and see who will be the first to turn his pipe darker."[25]

To those who most admired Taishō, this friendly informality was the essence of his character. Princess Nashimoto remarks in her memoirs: "In contrast to Emperor Meiji, Emperor Taishō was a very friendly, lighthearted person."[26] Bōjō Toshinaga writes in the same vein that Taishō "was an amiable person with a commoner-like [heiminteki] demeanor." Bōjō calls him Japan's first truly "human emperor [ningen tennō]."[27] To the extent that this was true in terms of his personal style, Taishō had the potential to forge a much more intimate relationship with his subjects than Meiji had ever en-joyed.

To his critics, however, who had greatly admired Meiji's far more dignified manner, Yoshihito's "common" attributes made him unforgivably vulgar in ways that threatened to di-minish the prestige and grandeur of the imperial house. A case in point was Yoshihito's residence, the Akasaka detached palace, which he had rebuilt in 1906 in a lavish European ro-coco style with a pink marble exterior, and which he fur-nished with mock Louis XV furniture. Everything about Yoshihito's "French house," as Meiji called it, seemed to mock the refined elegance of traditional Japanese styles favored by the court and the aristocracy. The immense two-story stone building "looked like the offspring of the mating of the Grand Chateau at Versailles and Buckingham Palace."[28]

Then there was Yoshihito's coarse habit of ordering atten-dants to find him a suitable woman for the night. Japan's lead-ers overlooked Meiji's sexual excesses because they respected him as a member of their own elite circle. In contrast, they did not respect Yoshihito and found his sexual demands, which he continued to make after becoming emperor, repugnant. Once, when Taishō asked Yamagata Aritomo to bring him a lover, Yamagata, who refused to be Taishō's pimp, curtly replied, "No, Your Majesty, that cannot be done."[29] Hara Kei, who had succeeded Saionji as president of the Seiyūkai in 1914 and who would become prime minister in 1918, wrote in his diary in 1916 that there had been many things about Crown Prince Yoshihito which people had not liked and this was still true now that he was emperor. Among them were his affairs with women. Hara noted that as a consequence Emperor Taishō was the subject of much derision at court and in the corridors of the Diet.[30]

Emperor Taishō and Politics

When Meiji died, the privy council met with Prime Minister Saionji and other members of his cabinet to select the new reign name. They chose "Taishō," or "Great Righteousness," which was based on a passage from an ancient Chinese text, *The Spring and Autumn Annals*. The term denoted imperial benevolence and as such, it indicated a desired continuity with the spirit of Meiji's reign. However, Taishō's first rescript, of August 1912, expressed fears that the Meiji legacy of national "wealth and power" could well be undone. It read in part, "In these days which are full of events both at home and abroad, We who have now acceded to the Throne, view them day and night with great concern and are anxious not to turn to naught the work bequeathed by the late Emperor."

The court was not unique in facing the future with anxiety. The journalist A. Morgan Young observed a general malaise in Japan after Meiji died, which he attributed to a pervasive sense of anticlimax: "Nearly half a century of intense activity had ended in a certain lassitude. Enthusiasm had spent itself and there was a reaction. Japan was settling down into a rut." As we will see, this malaise, accompanied by the "feeling that in the way before them the people lacked tried and trusted leaders,"[31] was deepened by the "Taishō Political Crisis" of 1912–13. To a lesser extent, it was also due to recent developments in China, where the implications for Japan of the 1911 Revolution were unclear. The Manchu dynasty had been overthrown but the new Republic was soon held hostage to warlordism. How far instability in China would threaten Japan's commercial interests there was unknown.

It was the Emperor's particular misfortune that the "Taishō Political Crisis" erupted so early in his reign. In brief, the crisis began when the army minister resigned on December 2, 1912, to protest the failure of the Saionji cabinet to endorse the army's plans for two new divisions. This forced Saionji and his cabinet to resign and led to Taishō's appointment of Katsura, Yamagata's choice as the next prime minister. However, the navy, fearing that Katsura would postpone its plans for expanding the fleet, refused to nominate a navy minister. Faced with this obstruction in organizing his cabinet, Katsura had Taishō issue an imperial order to the navy to cooperate. Only when the navy complied, on the understanding that both services would temporarily shelve their respective demands for military appropriations, did the Katsura cabinet take office.

Katsura, of course, publicly maintained that the imperial order was Taishō's idea, not his. But few believed him, and Katsura was widely attacked by opposition critics for blatantly abusing the emperor's prerogative of appointing ministers of state for his own (Katsura's) political gain. There quickly arose a "movement to protect constitutional government," which mobilized public opinion against Katsura. Since it was also thought that Yamagata was behind Katsura, Yamagata, too, came under attack. The informal, extra-constitutional power the *genrō* had always wielded was now a matter of increasing public ridicule in the press and in the streets.

Katsura, however, soon parted ways with Yamagata. Desperate to establish an independent power base of his own, he announced in January 1913 his plan to form a new party, the Dōshikai, which was launched on February 7 in Tokyo. This initiative alienated Yamagata, who was just as opposed to the party movement as he had always been. And it further alienated the Seiyūkai, whose domination of the house of representatives had forced Katsura's earlier cabinets to compromise on matters of national policy. The "Crisis" came to a boil early in February when the Seiyūkai, having accused Katsura of manipulating the throne, tabled a non-confidence motion against him in the Diet. Katsura responded belligerently by having Taishō suspend the Diet for five days. Since Prince Saionji, the Seiyūkai president, refused to withdraw the motion, Katsura again used Taishō to try and save his cabinet.

Accordingly, on February 9 Taishō summoned Saionji to the palace and told him that he was exceedingly concerned that Katsura and the Diet had arrived at this impasse. He then gave Saionji a rescript requesting that the non-confidence motion be withdrawn. Taken aback, Saionji later showed the rescript to the lord keeper of the privy seal, Prince Fushimi Sadanobu, who said he knew nothing about it. They saw that it did not bear the required counter-signature of a minister of state and concluded, quite rightly, that it must have been written by Katsura, although again Katsura later maintained that Taishō had acted on his own volition. Still, Saionji thought he ought to comply with what were ostensibly the emperor's wishes. When he recommended this course to the party, however, the Seiyūkai refused.[32]

The non-confidence motion had the active support of the press. For instance, in an article on February 11 entitled, "Katsura's Great Responsibility for Involving the Imperial House in Political Conflict," the *Jiji Shinpō* accused Katsura of exploiting the politically inexperienced Taishō in a manner that threatened to destroy constitutional government and demanded Katsura's immediate resignation.[33] Protesters in the swelling "movement to protect constitutional government" also demanded Katsura's resignation as they rioted in the streets, with several deaths resulting from clashes with the police. Ultimately, Katsura and his cabinet were forced to resign on February 20, bringing the "Taishō Political Crisis" to an end. In the aftermath, Katsura's successor, Admiral Yamamoto Gonnohyōe (Gonbei), who was recommended to Taishō by Yamagata with Saionji's blessing as well, would mend fences with the parties; in fact, Yamamoto's cabinet depended upon the support of the Seiyūkai.

The general significance of the "Taishō Political Crisis" is that it left the Seiyūkai with stronger leverage in national politics at the expense of Yamagata and other opponents of the parties. It also marked the greater political involvement of the people and the press. But more specifically, the "Crisis" had exposed the dangers of dragging the imperial institution into the political fray, where the authority of the throne could be easily manipulated by one side or the other. The court reacted quickly to this last reality three days after Katsura resigned. In order to uphold the separation of the court from the government, Taishō warned Imperial Household Minister Watanabe Chiaki not to linger in the room, as he had taken to doing, when the elder statesmen met at the palace.[34] This was only a minor change, but it shows a desire to maintain the political neutrality of the throne even in small ways.

In reviewing the circumstances that had led to his first

order, commanding the navy to furnish the Katsura cabinet with a navy minister, Taishō saw that the imperial house would always be subject to political manipulation as long as the army and navy could fell a cabinet by withdrawing or withholding a service minister. He was therefore determined to back Prime Minister Yamamoto when he moved to change the service regulations, allowing generals and admirals not on active duty to be appointed army minister and navy minister, respectively. To Taishō's credit, he supported Yamamoto even though it meant rebuffing Yamagata, who opposed this reform.[35]

However, Yamamoto resigned in April 1914 under intense public pressure for his involvement in the Siemens bribery scandal. Since Taishō had relied heavily upon Yamamoto to check Yamagata's influence, he repeatedly urged him to stay at his post, but to no avail. The emperor's respect for the Admiral was not reciprocated, however: Yamamoto later stated to Hara Kei that in his opinion Taishō was too inexperienced, too reticent, and too weak to hold his ground on important political issues.[36] Hara agreed, for it was obvious that Taishō was no match for Yamagata. Hara regretted that all Yamagata had to do in dealing with Taishō was to ask him for his opinions, cleverly pretend to defer to them, and then reinterpret them to suit his own interests while persuading the Emperor to approve of this or that course of action.[37] Hara was similarly critical of Ōkuma Shigenobu, who, backed by the Dōshikai, followed Yamamoto as prime minister in 1914. In Hara's opinion, Ōkuma used flattery and frequent references to conversations he had had with Meiji years ago to ingratiate himself with Taishō.[38]

Notwithstanding their many political differences, Hara and Yamagata agreed that Taishō's shallow judgment made him an ineffective emperor. This was their conclusion during a conversation in 1915 in which Hara asked Yamagata who would advise Taishō on the crucial matter of appointing prime ministers once the last of the original elder statesmen, including in particular Yamagata (then aged seventy-seven) and Matsukata Masayoshi (who was eighty), had died out. Yamagata had no clear answer, but for his part Hara thought Saionji, who had been admitted to the *genrō* circle following Katsura's downfall in 1913, could assist Taishō in the future, because Saionji had a strong sense of responsibility which transcended partisan politics.[39] And indeed, after Yamagata died on February 1, 1922, Saionji became the last *genrō*.

Ōkuma was in power when Taishō, as directed by the cabinet, issued an imperial rescript declaring war on Germany, on August 23, 1914. Taishō himself had been sympathetic to Germany, mostly because he had admired the Kaiser as a strong and resourceful sovereign. But the government was committed to entering World War I on the basis of the Anglo-Japanese Alliance, and in any case Taishō appears to have had little to do with the actual war decision, except to sanction it automatically, as was expected of him. Nor, for that matter, was Taishō involved in the opportunistic and largely unproductive "Twenty-One Demands," orchestrated by Ōkuma's Foreign Minister Katō Takaaki (Kōmei), against China in 1915. Taishō may have had his own opinion about this crude initiative, but the sources are unrevealing on this point, as they are on so many issues in his career.

It seems certain, however, that Taishō was personally

drawn to Ōkuma, and that after Yamamoto resigned, Taishō hoped Ōkuma might assist in keeping Yamagata at bay. Accordingly, once Ōkuma came under fire in the Diet from the Seiyūkai for the Twenty-One Demands and other wartime policies, Taishō was afraid he would resign and continually implored him not to do so.[40] In August 1915, Ōkuma prolonged his administration by having Katō resign instead, but in 1916 Ōkuma showed every sign that he wanted to retire along with his cabinet. Finally, on October 4 Ōkuma presented to Taishō his written resignation. Unusually, it included the recommendation that Katō be appointed as his successor.

This infuriated Yamagata, who asserted that Ōkuma's unprecedented attempt to name his own successor had violated the emperor's prerogative of appointing prime ministers. Yamagata had a point, but what really angered him was that Ōkuma had deliberately bypassed the *genrō* in recommending Katō. Yamagata therefore quickly reasserted his influence by insisting in a meeting of the elder statesmen that General Terauchi Masatake, from Chōshū, should be recommended to the Emperor. Taishō, discouraged by Ōkuma's resignation and unenthusiastic about Terauchi, nevertheless duly "commanded" Terauchi to form the next cabinet.[41] Clearly, Yamagata continued to dominate the court even though his power was gradually slipping to the parties in the country at large.

It was at about this time that Empress Sadako (Teimei) noticed a great change in Taishō. He had always been apprehensive about his ability to meet the high standards set by Meiji and thus, as she recalls, his "nature was to feel a strong sense of responsibility and whatever he did, he was very earnest."[42] At least he attempted to appear in control as he performed his official duties. For instance, he always stood up (as Meiji had usually done and as Shōwa would do later) while hearing his ministers report on state affairs. On one occasion during the War, the minister of communications in the Terauchi cabinet, Den Kenjirō, asked if Taishō would prefer to sit down since this would be a long and detailed report on wartime economic problems, which might take an hour. Taishō replied, "This is fine," and remained on his feet, motionless, while listening to what Den had to say.[43]

But the combined pressures of political intrigues at court and endless reports on Japan's wartime operations had caused him to become "a different person"—withdrawn, depressed, and very tired.[44] In 1917 and 1918 illness forced him to spend long periods away from his desk in the palace library where he worked. He was scarcely consulted when the government decided in August 1918 that Japan would participate in the Siberian Intervention, an Allied mission to cover the withdrawal from Vladivostok of Czech units that had fought their way across Russia in hopes of eventually rejoining the war in Europe. Ultimately, Japan sent many more troops than had been proposed, and the army defied the cabinet by expanding its operations far beyond Vladivostok to support "White" Russian elements fighting the Bolsheviks.[45]

By September, when the question of who would replace Terauchi as prime minister arose, Taishō's deepening passivity had made him more vulnerable than ever to political manipulation. The Terauchi cabinet had come to grief over its handling of the nationwide Rice Riots that summer; especially controversial was the government's use of troops to restore order in some regions where protests over the rising price of rice had spread beyond control. Anticipating Terauchi's downfall, Yamagata told Taishō he thought Saionji should be the next prime minister.[46] Although hard-pressed to recognize the growing political power of the Seiyūkai, Yamagata thought that Saionji was preferable to Hara, the Seiyūkai leader.

And so with Terauchi ill and his cabinet reeling under public pressure, Yamagata arranged for Taishō to summon Saionji to an audience at the palace on September 21, 1918, during which Taishō asked Saionji to stand by to form a cabinet and handed him a note to that effect. Saionji was surprised, for he had assumed that Taishō had simply wanted his views on who might succeed Terauchi; he himself had no desire to be prime minister again. He therefore said he needed time to consider Taishō's request and withdrew.

It will be recalled that Saionji had not known how to interpret Taishō's rescript in February 1913, during the "Taishō Political Crisis." He was no less perplexed by Taishō's note on this occasion. Showing it to Matsukata Masayoshi, who was then lord keeper of the privy seal, Saionji said that if it had the force of an imperial rescript, he would have no choice but to obey. But when they subsequently asked Imperial Household Minister Hatano Takano for his opinion, Hatano thought the note was not a formal rescript but only a private memorandum containing the personal views of the Emperor for the purposes of discussion. Matsukata reached the same conclusion and advised Saionji it would be appropriate to decline Taishō's request on the grounds of ill-health.[47]

Having rightly attributed Taishō's intervention to Yamagata's influence, Saionji decided to reply to Taishō exactly as Matsukata had advised, for he knew that Yamagata would then have to accept Hara as the next prime minister. At this point Yamagata finally capitulated, but when Terauchi resigned at the end of September, Yamagata still could not bring himself to recommend Hara to Taishō and asked Saionji to do so instead.[48] Hara thus became the first Japanese prime minister to lead a majority party cabinet while also holding a seat in the lower house of the Diet.

The Formation of the Taishō Regency

Taishō was too fatigued to attend the opening of the Diet in December 1918, and his health continued to decline in early 1919, with sciatica forcing him to miss the annual Kigensetsu observances in February. He attended the grand military maneuvers that autumn but soon afterward experienced the first of several debilitating strokes. As a result, he found it impossible to walk without stumbling, to talk without slurring his words, and to maintain his train of thought. His memory was also impaired.

On November 8, 1919, after hearing a medical report on Taishō's condition, Prime Minister Hara doubted whether Taishō was capable of reading aloud even the shortest imperial rescripts on important state occasions.[49] Anticipating that Crown Prince Hirohito would eventually have to take over Taishō's ceremonial duties, Hara began to think in terms of sending Hirohito on a tour of Europe to broaden his experience. Meanwhile, it was agreed that Taishō's public appearances should be kept to a minimum and that any audiences he held should be cut short if he appeared to falter. Taishō did have occasional good days, but henceforth he increasingly re-treated with the empress to the imperial villas at Hayama, Numazu, or Nikkō, where, except for brief and infrequent appearances at court, they largely remained until he died at Hayama on December 25, 1926.

In retrospect, Taishō's disabilities by themselves probably did not necessitate a regency. The crown prince could have performed Taishō's ceremonial duties and the government could have obtained Taishō's formal sanction for its policies simply by "reporting" its decisions to him. In fact it had been doing that already. Other factors persuaded the government that a regency was necessary.

Firstly, Japan's leaders were alarmed by Taishō's decline because it occurred at a time when, following the 1917 Russian Revolution and the recent collapse of long-established monarchies in postwar Europe, monarchies everywhere, including Japan, seemed very vulnerable to sweeping change. In Japan the sudden upsurge of wartime labor strikes, the upheaval of the Rice Riots, the spreading appeal of anarchism and Marxism in intellectual circles, and the emergence of a small but politicized labor union movement, all conveyed the impression that a rising tide of social and political radicalism might well engulf the imperial house. Moreover, the zeal of an expanding press in reporting these developments made public opinion, including opinion concerning the imperial house, an increasingly significant force in national affairs. In this context, given the imperative of reviving public respect for the imperial house, Japan's elites were disturbed by apparent changes in the way the people perceived Emperor Taishō.

In particular, they were apprehensive about widespread

public rumors to the effect that Taishō had sometimes behaved quite strangely: how, for instance, when opening a session of the Diet, he had once peered at everyone present through a rolled-up text of his rescript as if it were a telescope; or how, when greeting a foreign envoy who bowed before him in audience, he had rudely remarked on his visitor's bald pate. These stories are impossible to confirm but to Japan's elites they made Taishō a comic figure in the public eye and confirmed the general impression that he was simply unfit to rally public respect for the throne, as Meiji had done so successfully in his day.[50]

Secondly, some of Japan's leading politicians, including most notably Prime Minister Hara, were concerned that Taishō's poor health made him all the more susceptible to manipulation by the army and navy chiefs of staff, who frequently used their right of direct access to the throne to circumvent the cabinet and usurp the emperor's constitutional prerogatives in military matters. In 1920, for example, aware that the army had only to "report" its policies to the emperor to obtain his sanction, Hara suspected that the army chief of staff wanted to bring down his cabinet by unilaterally obtaining Taishō's approval for the resignation of Army Minister Tanaka Giichi, because Hara had opposed appropriations sought by the army. Hara felt that Emperor Meiji would not have allowed this to happen, but the weak-willed Emperor Taishō was another matter.[51]

Thirdly, there was the expectation, dating from the Meiji period, that the emperor should render his formal sanction on the basis of an informed opinion, following probing "imperial questions" (*gokamon*) that reflected the national interest. This process no longer applied to Taishō if indeed it ever had. His mind was too muddled, and he was away from court most of the time, removing him from the process of "working through the court" to declare the imperial will. Because "The loss of the Meiji Emperor and the illness of the Taishō Emperor removed one element of the consensus-making machinery which had developed since the Restoration,"[52] the monarchy had reached a point of crisis which only a regency could overcome.

As far as can be determined, the creation of a regency was first mentioned by Matsukata in a conversation with Hara on June 18, 1920. Hara welcomed the idea but wanted time to prepare the people for the regency and to groom Hirohito for his approaching responsibilities.[53] Responding to public rumors of Taishō's decline, the imperial household ministry had published in March a report on his condition. Other reports would follow in the press: in July 1920, April 1921, and October 1921.[54] Each was more specific than the last in detailing Taishō's troubles when speaking and walking, and his lapses of concentration. These problems were usually attributed not to strokes, which were the more likely cause, but to the residual effects of his childhood meningitis.

Time was also needed to forge a broad elite consensus in favor of a regency. Here, Saionji was not a problem, for he had concluded that Taishō could no longer carry out the duties of his office. Saionji was ready to help bring about a regency through his political ally Makino Nobuaki, who was appointed imperial household minister in February 1921.

Nor was there a problem with Yamagata, who had long regarded Taishō as second-rate. Rather, time was needed to

persuade the princes who served on the imperial family council and Empress Sadako that Taishō's disabilities made a regency inevitable. The imperial princes readily agreed, but at
first the Empress, who was a formidable person in her own
right, withheld her approval. She finally accepted the idea but
sharply criticized the government's frank public revelations of
Taishō's infirmities as impugning the dignity of the throne.[55]
Shikama Kōsuke, Taishō's naval aide-de-camp, felt the same
way. He reacted to the fourth medical report by writing in his
diary on October 4, 1921: "It is terrible for such newspapers as
the *Yomiuri* to stir things up with erroneous reports that the
Emperor is seriously ill." Blaming Imperial Household Minister Makino for releasing this report, he added, "In truth, there
are no exceptionally rapid changes in the Emperor's state of
health."[56] This last observation was probably accurate, in that
Taishō's decline in mind and body had been gradual, and
there were still times when he was lucid. But these were at
best unpredictable and short-lived. For the most part he was
disoriented and incoherent.

In 1920 and 1921 the process of forming a regency was further delayed by protracted disputes at court over two other issues. The first was whether Nagako, the daughter of Prince
Kuni Kunihiko of Satsuma, would be a suitable wife for
Crown Prince Hirohito. She had been selected without difficulty in January 1918, but the specific problem at hand in this
"Serious Court Incident," as it was known, was the disovery in
1920 of color-blindness in her mother's family, the Shimazu.
Yamagata in particular agreed with the opinion of scientists
who had been consulted that the purity of the imperial line
would be compromised if Nagako were to transmit this

hereditary condition to a future heir to the throne. He and others at court who shared this view therefore opposed Nagako's selection. One writer claims, unfortunately without presenting evidence, that when the matter was put before Taishō and the empress, Taishō, who had appeared to be off in a dream-world of his own, suddenly declared, "I hear that even science is fallible"[57] to the surprise of everyone present. If this is true, in a moment of lucidity Taishō personally approved Nagako, as had the empress. When Nagako's engagement to Hirohito was ultimately reconfirmed by the court in February 1921, Yamagata felt obliged to apologize to Taishō and the Empress for having stood in the way, and even offered his resignation as president of the privy council.[58] The offer was refused.

The second contentious issue had to do with whether Crown Prince Hirohito should go to Europe, as Hara had proposed. The empress felt it would be unwise given Taishō's ill health. Many conservative nationalists adamantly objected that Hirohito might be harmed by Korean terrorists, seizing this opportunity to demonstrate their opposition to Korea's annexation. There were protest demonstrations and pledges by some right-wing groups to block Hirohito's departure. However, Hara persisted with his proposal and on March 3, 1921 Hirohito departed with a large retinue on the cruiser *Katori* for an overseas tour that lasted until September 3. While stopping in Hong Kong and Singapore en route to Europe, he was equipped with no less than two bullet-proof vests, presumably to protect him from Korean gunmen.[59]

The issues of color-blindness in Nagako's family and Hirohito's European tour notwithstanding, by September 1921 the arrangements for a regency—reported to Hirohito soon after he returned to Japan—were well in hand, including an agreement that when in Tokyo the emperor and empress would continue to live in the imperial palace, while the crown prince regent would remain at the Akasaka detached palace. Not even Hara's shocking assassination by a demented youth on November 4 was allowed to disrupt the realization of a regency. On the morning of November 25, the imperial family council, chaired by Crown Prince Hirohito, unanimously approved his appointment as regent. After this was unanimously confirmed by the privy council that afternoon, an imperial edict (*shokushō*) was issued, bearing Hirohito's and Taishō's seals and the names of Imperial Household Minister Makino, the new prime minister Takahashi Korekiyo, and the members of his cabinet. The edict informed the country that owing to the emperor's ill health the crown prince had been appointed regent. The next day a fifth medical report was published, detailing Taishō's mental and physical decline, which, as before, was attributed to the long-term effects of his childhood meningitis.[60]

Before Hara died, he and Makino had debated whether they should have replicas made of Emperor Taishō's seals, which suggests they anticipated that Taishō might somehow resist the establishment of a regency.[61] How far Taishō himself had sensed what was going on is unknown, but he probably understood that he had been "abandoned," as Shikama put it, when Taishō was informed on November 25 that Hirohito had been appointed regent. Shikama tells us in his diary that when Grand Chamberlain Ogimachi Sanemasa came to Taishō's quarters to obtain his box of seals that morning, Taishō refused to hand it over, stating that he would prefer to give it to the chief aide-de-camp. Later, on December 8, Shikama further records that Taishō told him, "I am not that ill." "The Emperor himself," Shikama commented, "does not see that he is particularly ill."[62] The inference here is that the regency resulted from a palace coup.

It can indeed be seen as a palace coup in a broad sense, in that power at court shifted decisively from Yamagata to Prince Saionji Kinmochi, who, with Hara earlier and then through Makino Nobuaki, had initiated the regency and who now served as the regent's chief adviser. For Saionji, the creation of the regency was a kind of "Taishō Restoration," that is, an opportunity to revive Meiji's legacy by restoring the integrity of the emperor's constitutional prerogatives, the abuse of which had been the hallmark of Taishō's career. As his English biographer writes, Saionji saw the regency as "a means of protecting the political role of the Court and Japan's polity as a constitutional monarchy."[63]

But Taishō's "retirement" (there was no provision in the imperial house law for an emperor's abdication) was not a coup in the strict sense, for the procedures which were followed on November 25 all complied with article nineteen of the imperial house law, which stipulated that when the emperor could not function because of a permanent condition, "a Regency shall be instituted with the advice of the Imperial Family Council and with that of the Privy Council." Article twenty further stated the "Regency shall be assumed by the Crown Prince." Moreover, virtually everyone of any political consequence—save Taishō himself—wished for Taishō retirement: the cabinet, the *genrō*, the empress, the imperial princes, the privy council, and Crown Prince Hirohito.

Reviving the Taishō Monarchy: Hirohito as Regent

Upon becoming crown prince regent, the twenty-year-old Hirohito was emperor in all but name, and Taishō emperor in name only. Hirohito immediately assumed Taishō's ceremonial functions (some of which he had already assumed earlier), such as opening the Diet, greeting foreign visitors, and attending military maneuvers. He also took over all of Taishō's political duties at court, including the appointment of prime ministers and the sanctioning of government policies with the formal imperial will. The personal attributes and political perceptions which Hirohito brought to his responsibilities as regent and later as emperor will be explored in the next chapter. Here, our main concern is what the regency generally meant for the late Taishō monarchy.

Under the guidance of Saionji and Makino, Hirohito carried out his political responsibilities effectively. In May 1922 Saionji expressed to Prime Minister Takahashi his personal satisfaction that the regent was making very good progress in acting on Taishō's behalf.[64] To foreshadow a key theme in the next chapter, Hirohito trusted Saionji and shared Saionji's conception of constitutional monarchy. Consequently, in contrast to Taishō's troubled relationship with Yamagata, Hirohito cooperated with Saionji without feeling manipulated by him, ensuring the orderly transition from one cabinet to another. When the Takahashi cabinet fell in June 1922, for instance, after less than a year in office, Hirohito readily followed Saionji's advice in appointing Admiral Katō Tomosaburō as prime minister, and when Katō resigned, he did likewise in appointing Admiral Yamamoto Gonnohyōe on September 2, 1923. The circumstances of Yamamoto's installation were scarcely propitious. The day before, a great earthquake had struck the Kantō region, leaving over 100,000 people dead and two million homeless. Yet Hirohito managed to stay calm as he performed the installation ceremony on the grounds of the Akasaka detached palace "with the embers of Tokyo still burning round them and the earth still trembling with the after-quakes."[65]

Hirohito also kept his composure following an attempt on his life in the "Toranomon Incident," which occurred on December 23, 1923. That day, as the regent's car passed through the Toranomon district of Tokyo, Nanba Daisuke, a young self-proclaimed Communist sympathizer, stepped from the crowd and fired a gun at the regent. The bullet missed Hirohito but shattered the car window and wounded a chamberlain in the face. The police immediately seized Nanba, who would later be tried, convicted, and executed for high treason. Meanwhile, the regent's car sped on to the Diet, where Hirohito, appearing unruffled, proceeded to open the new parliamentary session. For this composure he was widely praised by government leaders and the press.[66]

After this, the newspapers and magazines took to publishing photographs of the bespectacled regent seated at his desk, looking intently at the reader over an open book. These photographs projected Hirohito as a man of probity, competence, and self-assurance, one who could be relied upon to perform the political functions of constitutional monarchy. This impression in turn helped to align the imperial house with contemporary political trends, which to many Japanese reflected "the normal course of constitutional government" in the post-war 1920s. Japan seemed to be developing a more open political system, typified by intense electoral competiton between the Seiyūkai and the Kenseikai (formerly the Dōshikai; renamed the Minseitō in 1927). After a hiatus of several short-lived bureaucratic cabinets, the appointment in 1925 of Katō Takaaki's Kenseikai cabinet marked the return of party government, which would last, with the two major parties alternating in power, until May 1932. Another big step towards greater political pluralism was taken when the Katō cabinet, responding to popular pressure, successfully sponsored a bill to give all males aged twenty-five or older the right to vote. This opened the door to the political participation of new social democratic parties supported by labor and tenant farmer organizations.

Against this background of rising democratic expectations, it is significant that Hirohito also did much to restore public respect for the imperial institution by promoting a new popular image of the monarchy. Of course, he did not do this by himself. The imperial household ministry, the cabinet, and especially the media all had a hand in this continuing public relations exercise.

The crown prince first emerged, rather surprisingly, as a "media star" during his European tour, when the English press constantly referred to him as the "young Prince" from Japan. Japanese newspapers and magazines were quick to use the same term in reporting the highlights of his tour. This media coverage was very thorough. In late 1921, for instance, a special issue of *Fujin gahō* (Women's Graphic) provided readers with a detailed narrative of Hirohito's engagements, related essays by Japanese officials who accompanied him, numerous photographs, and a color map of his route from Japan to Europe.

Specifically, among other things, the magazine covered Hirohito's ride with King George V in a horse-drawn carriage from Victoria Station to Buckingham Palace, where he would stay for several nights; his meeting with Prime Minister Lloyd George; his visits to Parliament and to Oxford University, as well as the Universities of Cambridge and Edinburgh, where he received honorary degrees; and the ceremonies in which he was made an honorary field marshal in the British army and a Knight of the Garter (these particular honors were withdrawn during World War II). Hirohito's ensuing tour of World War I battlefields on the continent, his meetings with King Victor Emmanuel and Pope Benedict XV in Rome, and other such highlights were also reported in much detail. Throughout, it was noted that Hirohito carried himself with a dignity and confidence that belied his age and political experience. As Hara stated in his diary, "The trip was a huge success and the imperial family and Japan will benefit from it in the future."[67]

While in Britain, Hirohito was much impressed by the strength of public affection for King George. Moreover, after a banquet hosted in Scotland by the Duke of Atholl, during which members of the aristocracy mixed freely with their servants, local farmers, and shepherds, he was heard to say, "How nice it would be if the imperial family could do something like this, to get into direct touch with the people."[68] Accordingly, soon after his return to Japan, it was predicted in the Japanese press that he "would banish all caution" in bringing the imperial house closer to the people in ways that characterized "modern" monarchies in postwar Europe, especially Britain.[69]

Hirohito did not quite "banish all caution" in this regard, but as regent he did simplify some of the elaborate protocol used at court, dropping the use of imperial honorifics on certain formal occasions and, to attune the monarchy to "modern" social ways, improving the living and working conditions of ladies-in-waiting at the Akasaka detached palace. In the aftermath of the great Kantō earthquake he also toured devestated areas near the palace,[70] donated money to earthquake victims, and opened the grounds of Ueno Park to provide temporary shelter for the homeless. In several rescripts he expressed his profound sympathy for the people, and he postponed his wedding ceremony, which had been scheduled for November, as a further sign of this sympathy. All of these initiatives, which were widely reported in the press, were meant to demonstrate the imperial virtues of compassion and benevolence that had been closely associated with the monarchy in the Meiji era.

The Toranomon Incident led to heightened police security for the Regent, and this prevented him from mixing with the people as he might have wished. Yet thanks to extensive media coverage, Hirohito increasingly symbolized the mood of change and the eagerness to experiment with new lifestyles, which characterized much of postwar Japanese urban society. Despite the postwar recession, a vibrant consumer culture stimulated by an expanding advertising industry flourished during the 1920s in Japan's big cities, including Tokyo and Yokohama as they were being rebuilt after the earthquake. Western fashions were all the rage—ranging from jazz, classical music, drama, films, and dance revues to "Chaplin caramels" and such manifestations of the "good life" as the wireless, new kitchen appliances, and (for the wealthy) cars.

In this setting Hirohito came across as a "modern" representative of the imperial house who, dressed nattily in plus-fours, liked to play golf, a sport he had discovered while in Britain, and who pursued his interest in marine biology, using a new laboratory that had been built specially for him. The "modern" face of the Taishō Regency was also evident when Hirohito and Nagako were married on January 26, 1924. The couple wore traditional dress for the private Shintō rituals conducted at the imperial palace. But as A. Morgan Young observed, "Afterward came the great concession to modernism, when the wedded pair, in European dress, the Princess wearing a coronet, drove together to the Akasaka palace, through streets lined with soldiers and with multitudes of cheering school children, who now and then, also departing from tradition, which prescribed perfect silence, broke into cheers."[71]

Not until the wedding in 1959 of Crown Prince Akihito and Miss Shōda Michiko, the present emperor and empress, did the Japanese people again celebrate the rejuvenation of the monarchy so demonstratively. The parallel is worth noting, for just as Hirohito and Nagako symbolized the revitalization of the Taishō monarchy when Emperor Taishō was ill and virtually overlooked, so too did Akihito and his bride personify the remaking of the postwar Shōwa monarchy, when Emperor Hirohito was too associated with the recent war and

Japan's defeat to do so himself convincingly.

After their marriage the crown prince and princess were constantly in the news. In May 1924, for instance, the press reported that several members of their household staff at the Akasaka palace had fallen ill with typhus, which was then sweeping the capital. To ensure the safety of the imperial couple, High Steward Chinda Sutemi had the entire palace disinfected.[72] In 1925 the press similarly catered to public concern for the crown princess during a long and difficult pregnancy, until it was announced on December 7 that at last she had given birth to a baby girl, Princess Shigeko. This news led to spirited public celebrations throughout Japan, although many Japanese would have been even happier had the child been a male who would one day inherit the throne.[73]

Thus, through extensive media publicity the regent and his immediate family emerged as symbols of an updated and more publicly accessible imperial house, and to this extent Hirohito helped to popularize and revive the monarchy as Emperor Taishō, with his "commoner-like" instincts, might have done had he not been overwhelmed by illness and the burdens of emperorship.

The Death of Emperor Taishō

Hirohito's popularization, however, was only one strand in the rejuvenation of the late Taishō monarchy. Another was a militant imperial loyalism advocated by conservatives in the bureaucracy, the Peers, the military, and indeed significant elements in the "established" parties, who were determined to exalt the imperial house, if not Emperor Taishō himself, as the fountainhead of Japanese nationalism. The cabinet and some constitutional monarchists at court (notably Makino Nobuaki) were likewise caught up in this enterprise to varying degrees.

In brief, late Taishō loyalism was largely a reaction to the perceived spread of "dangerous thoughts" following the formation of the Japanese Communist Party in July 1922. Because the Communists, supported by the Comintern in Moscow, advocated the revolutionary overthrow of the "emperor system" and the capitalist order, imperial loyalists were obsessed with defending the imperial house from the threat posed by the likes of Nanba Daisuke after the Toranomon Incident. General Tanaka Giichi, for one, is a good illustration of this obsession. He almost certainly had this threat in mind when he addressed a national meeting of the Imperial Reservists' Association in January 1924. Referring to the imperial wedding that month, Tanaka declared,

> We who are bathed in the glory of celebrating this felicitous event truly have received the benevolence of the throne. Our exalted nation whose glory flows from its national polity based on an unbroken imperial reign is one which has no parallel in the world. Our duty is to *protect* this national polity, *defend* this glorious nation and expand Japan's power and prestige eternally throughout the world.[74]

This defensive mentality in late Taishō loyalism is evident in the enactment of the peace preservation law in 1925, which prescribed heavy penalties for anyone convicted of plotting to overthrow the *kokutai*, or "national polity." Aimed primarily at the small but feared Communist movement, the new law

enabled the government to pursue the Communists relent-
lessly. Tanaka, as prime minister (he was first appointed in
April 1927 and then re-elected in February 1928), invoked this
law when mounting a nationwide crackdown on them in
March 1928.

Besides *kokutai*, leading loyalists habitually used such
terms as *ōdō*, the "kingly way," and *kōdō*, the "imperial way,"
when extolling the imperial house as the pillar of the nation.
To cite but one example, at Tanaka's first press conference
after being elected chairman of the Seiyūkai in 1925, he went
out of his way to advocate the importance of "spiritual education" (*seishin kyōiku*) in advancing "the politics of the kingly
way based on the unity of the sovereign and the people (*kun-
min itchi no ōdō seiji*)."[5] Tanaka and other conservatives meant
by this a spiritual unity which depended upon the symbolic
distancing of the imperial house to a point "above the clouds"
where the imperial house and the state would command the
unqualified loyalty of the people. As it turned out, Taishō's
death in 1926 provided the perfect ritual occasion to promote
this idealized vision of the monarchy on a national scale. Manipulated to the very end, Taishō ironically did more in death
to enhance the prestige of the monarchy than he had ever
done in life.

Following his retirement in 1921 Taishō seldom visited
Tokyo, and only then when his health allowed. He and the
Empress were there in May 1925 to celebrate their twenty-
fifth wedding anniversary. After a banquet at the palace
which was hosted by the crown prince regent, members of the
imperial family and other distinguished guests were taken to
the throne room to pay their respects to Taishō and the em-

press, who were waiting there for them.

Taishō subsequently went to Nikkō but in December returned to Tokyo, where, ten days after the birth of his grand-
daughter Princess Shigeko, he suddenly collapsed from a
stroke in his bathroom. He soon suffered another stroke, and
it was not until August 1926 that he was judged well enough
to be moved to Hayama, where his condition was further aggravated, first by bronchitis and then by pneumonia. In early
December he suffered another stroke which left him completely bedridden and able to eat only small helpings of ice
cream. His physicians and nurses were allowed to touch him
(in contrast to Meiji's treatment), but despite intensive medical
care, his condition quickly deteriorated.

From December 10, the imperial household ministry
published daily reports in the press and over the wireless of
his temperature, pulse rate, and other bodily functions. At
Hayama and elsewhere the police were mobilized to maintain
public order, and the Imperial Reservists staged mass vigils to
pray for his recovery. A mood of self-restraint (jishuku) took
hold as weddings, concerts, public meetings, and sporting con-
tests were postponed. Labor strikes were suspended or hastily
settled out of respect for Taishō. There were even several sui-
cides reported, apparently motivated by sympathy toward
him.[76]

As Taishō lay dying, the media, prompted by the imperial
household ministry, typically cast the regent in the role of the
loyal son, standing watch with the empress at Taishō's bed-
side, where they nursed him with cups of water until he finally died in the early hours of December 25 at the age of
forty-seven. This contrived tableau powerfully combined the

affection for the imperial house which Hirohito's earlier pop-ularization had nurtured and the feelings of awe which char-acterized Taishō imperial loyalism. The effect of such imagery was to highlight the imperial family as symbols of an idealized "family state" (*kazoku kokka*).[77] This symbolism was, of course, not new. Yet its intense projection by the mass media gave it an impetus which surpassed even the emotional force of the Meiji imperial cult. In this sense, although the in-stitutional foundations of the "emperor system" were laid in the Meiji period, the modern dynamics of its mass appeal date more from the mid-1920s.

After two days of funeral rites on February 7–8, Taishō's remains were buried in the Musashino Imperial Mausoleum to the west of the capital. Most Japanese were caught up in grief for Taishō, at least to some extent, not because they had admired or identified with him as an individual but simply because he had been emperor, whom death now ennobled. Yet there were also Japanese who cared little about the year of of-ficial mourning, which flowed into the government's elabo-rate preparations for Emperor Shōwa's formal enthronement ceremonies in November 1928 in Kyoto. Therefore, the gov-ernment deemed it necessary to suppress any public activity that contradicted the nation's solemn observances as Japan rit-ually reconfirmed the institutional charisma and historical continuity of the imperial house in the Taishō-Shōwa transi-tion. During official ritual events in this period, even trivial displays of public indifference were prohibited. People who played "frivolous music," who held raucous parties in city parks, or who went on rowdy train excursions and so forth were routinely arrested by the police.[78]

Foreign observers could not help but notice this coercive atmosphere. Concerning the Shintō rites and public displays of loyalty at the time of Shōwa's enthronement in Kyoto, the Swiss envoy to Japan wrote:

> The Emperor himself did not … want all that panoply. The court and government forced it on him. The [government's] stage-management was efficient but sadly untalented, mechanical. The crowds [marshalled by the police], passive; not a quiver of enthusiasm or of pride. Contrast such occasions in Berlin, London, Madrid, or even the republics. I felt not a moment's emotion. [Official] Japanese utterances reminded [me] rather of the former affection in Russia for the "Little father the Tsar."[79]

Greatly esteemed and almost larger than life, Emperor Meiji would have been a hard act to follow for anyone, much less his son and heir, Yoshihito. The fact that by the time Meiji died, intense interest in the monarchy had made the office of emperor "public property"[80] meant that Taishō would be subject to growing public scrutiny and his flaws would be widely known sooner or later, if not at the very beginning of his reign. The notion in nationalist ideology that the emperor was a "manifest deity" did not necessarily connote his absolute perfection, only that the emperor should aspire to, and broadly symbolize, the highest possible moral and political standards. Taishō was not "mad" as such. However, his poor health, weakness of character, and eccentric behavior made him a parody of this ideal. Hence the Taishō Regency was created, to mark a new beginning for the monarchy in the 1920s.

More specifically, Taishō was "retired" in 1921 because he was judged inadequate in the face of significant political and social changes, including Japan's international position, that occurred during his early reign. Politically, the escalating struggle for power between the *genrō* and the parties, as well as the increasing political assertiveness of the military, put a high premium on the emperor's capacity to referee conflict and ensure elite consensus in declaring the imperial will. Meiji had found this difficult to do, but for the most part succeeded because he was respected by all concerned. But Taishō, held in contempt by Yamagata on the one hand and Hara and Saionji on the other, found it impossible. They wanted an emperor whom they could trust in the process of "working through the court" to get things done politically. Whether the regent, substituting for Taishō, could meet this need was uncertain in 1921. But even untried, Hirohito was seen as a better bet than his ailing and incompetent father.

Taishō was also regarded as a liability to the throne because he proved unable to symbolize national unity when wartime and postwar Japan was swept by unprecedented social conflict manifested in the Rice Riots, the rise of new social protest movements, and new ideologies of "liberation" through reform or revolution. Convinced that unless the monarchy cultivated greater public support it would remain vulnerable to possible subversion and to rising indifference, the founders of the regency looked to the "young Prince" Hirohito to appeal to a broader cross-section of society.

Nor, finally, was Taishō a compelling public symbol of national pride as Japan emerged from World War I as one of the five great powers in the new League of Nations. This was yet another reason for his "retirement" in 1921, when his reign effectively ended and when Hirohito's effectively began. Unlike medieval Japanese emperors who abdicated and then exerted immense political influence as "retired" emperors (*insei*), Taishō simply disappeared from the political scene. Although he was briefly remembered when the nation mourned his death, soon thereafter he was once again forgotten, this time for good.

Emperor Meiji in 1872. This was his first formal photograph.

Emperor Meiji in 1874.

Emperor Meiji reviewing the troops.

Crown Prince Yoshihito, on the occasion of his visit in 1910 to Koki-an, belonging to Yamagata Aritomo (front, left).

Emperor Taishō reviewing a military parade.

Crown Prince Hirohito and King George V during Hirohito's visit to Britain in 1921.

General Douglas MacArthur and Emperor Shōwa at their first meeting, on September 27, 1945.

Emperor Shōwa on the Kyōyama Highway, February 19, 1945, during one of his postwar tours.

Emperor Shōwa and the Empress during their visit to Disneyland, on October 8, 1975.

The present Emperor and Empress with President and Mrs. Clinton.

SHŌWA
(HIROHITO)

•

The "Reprieved"
Emperor

Crown Prince Hirohito on November 25, 1921,
the day he took office as Regent.

Hirohito began his reign of Shōwa, or "illustrious peace," by proclaiming high hopes for the future. In his first rescript, promulgated on December 28, 1926, he declared, "The world is now in a process of evolution…. A new chapter is being opened in the history of civilization." He went on:

> This nation's settled policy always stands for progress and improvement. Simplicity instead of vain display, originality instead of blind imitation, progress in view of this period of evolution, improvement to keep pace with the advancement of civilization, national harmony in purpose and in action, beneficence to all classes of people, and friendship to all the nations of the earth: these are the cardinal aims to which Our most profound and abiding solicitude is directed.

However, domestic conflict, not "harmony," and enmity with other nations, not "friendship," soon made a mockery of these naive expectations, and Shōwa himself would mostly be remembered for war, not peace. The historian Inoue Kiyoshi writes, "The man Hirohito was no doubt a sympathetic and courteous gentleman to his family and advisers. But Emperor Hirohito reigned at the summit of an atrocious emperor system fascism and continued to direct both aggressive wars and a system which oppressed the people."[1] Or, as the Japanese Communist Party was reported by *The New York Times* as stating on January 8, 1989, the day after Shōwa's death: "We are called upon to speak out in deep emotion of the tens of millions of victims of the war of aggression and harsh domestic rule who cannot speak any more. The Emperor Hirohito bears the heaviest and supreme responsibility for the war of aggression."

From these perspectives, Shōwa's reprieve by General Douglas MacArthur, who exempted him from trial as a war criminal after World War II, was a momentous travesty of justice. In view of the emotions generated by Japan's aggression in the early Shōwa period, it is understandable that many people see Hirohito as a war criminal who regrettably "got away." But just how far was he in fact responsible for war? We have already begun to think about him in the context of the Taishō Regency. It remains to probe further into who he was and what part he played in twentieth-century Japanese and world history.

Hirohito's Personality and World View

Soon after his birth on April 29, 1901 Hirohito was given over to the care of a retired naval officer, Kawamura Sumiyoshi, and his wife. When Kawamura died in 1904, the child rejoined his parents at the Akasaka palace. How close he felt to them is difficult to say, but Kanroji Osanaga, one of his attendants, suggests that the Prince felt a special affection for Meiji and liked to "snuggle up" to "Granddaddy," as Hirohito called him, on the rare occasions when he visited Meiji at the imperial palace.[2] In return, Meiji gave him presents and smiled at him, although he said little to his grandson, just as he seldom spoke to Yoshihito. Over the years, Hirohito would identify strongly with Meiji as his political model.

Physically, young Hirohito was unimpressive. Being nearsighted, he had to wear glasses from an early age, and his attendants constantly tried to correct his poor posture. He was moreover a very awkward child who had difficulty buttoning his uniform. Calisthenics, horseback riding, swimming, and other exercises helped to improve his coordination, but in adulthood he remained an ungainly figure. When the Prince of Wales visited Japan in 1922, the crown prince invited him to a game of golf. So that his host would not be embarrassed, Edward found it necessary to feign "a disastrous hook" after seeing that Hirohito had trouble hitting the ball.[3]

From early on, Hirohito had what Baelz called a "quiet and retiring" nature,[4] especially in comparison with his next oldest and more exuberant brother, Chichibu. When Hirohito played tag with Chichibu and his second brother, Takamatsu, he "always played strictly according to the rules, never employing any of the little tricks that were possible in this game."[5] This tendency was one of his most important characteristics: in later years, he rigidly adhered to the "rules" of the political system as he understood them. But otherwise, he was generally passive, indecisive, and tended to avoid confrontation. Just before he died in January 1929, Empress Nagako's father told her: "The Emperor is weak-willed. Therefore, it is necessary for the Empress to assist him. Keep up your spirits."[6]

As an adult Hirohito's inclination was to endure, rather than to try boldly to change political situations he could not control, and this tendency likewise dates from his childhood. Among the court's guidelines for educating Hirohito was the instruction "to train him to endure hardships and difficulties" and "not to be selfish or wilful." These themes, and the importance of a disciplined sense of duty, were emphasized by General Nogi Maresuke, who was principal of the Peers' School when Hirohito began formal studies there in 1908. Nogi sought to instill in Hirohito the austere ethos of the former samurai class which the General exemplified in his own personal life. In 1975 Hirohito recalled that Nogi once admonished him always to walk to class, rain or shine. Nogi, he said, advocated "a very frugal, strenuous, self-disciplined life. That made a profound impression on me."[7] As emperor, Hirohito often stood deliberately unprotected in the rain while reviewing the troops.

For a brief period while he was regent, Hirohito departed from Nogi's model of a "strenuous, self-disciplined life." Shōwa later attributed this to the influence of his European tour, saying, "I knew freedom as a man for the first time in England."[8] Some of his advisers thought the "young Prince" was much too "high collar" in his frivolous preoccupation with playing golf in the mornings and bridge at night, and Prince Saionji (who himself had a reputation for living the high life as a youth) once felt it necessary to reprimand Hirohito for a boisterous party he had given at the Akasaka palace soon after returning from Europe. Saionji was annoyed because Hirohito and his guests, including friends from the Peers' School, had behaved in a loud undignified manner while drinking whisky (a gift from the Duke of Atholl) and listening to phonograph records.[9]

Yet Hirohito's "high collar" ways were only a youthful passing fancy. His underlying temperament was deeply conservative, indeed puritanical. Hirohito avoided alcohol, tobacco, and the sort of womanizing for which his grandfather and father were famous. His personal pleasures were few, including the game of mah jong, listening to music, and writing poetry, mostly in the *waka* genre. Poetry was probably his favorite pastime. Besides writing poems himself, he was fully familiar with Meiji's poems, which he admired greatly and which he sometimes quoted in political discussions to express his own point of view. This habit of speaking indirectly, through poetry or by making vague oracular pronouncements, was very typical of Emperor Shōwa.

Another personal interest which continued throughout his life was a fascination with the natural world. Prince Chichibu remembered that when Hirohito was about ten years old, they once went collecting insects. Chichibu soon grew bored with this activity, but Hirohito kept working meticulously: "From beginning to end, no matter how many insects there were, he carefully checked and recorded the name of each one."[10] Soon, Hirohito turned to marine biology, especially to the study of hydrozoa. He eventually published extensively on this subject, which in later years prompted the press to call him the "scientist-emperor" (*kagakusha tennō*). But Shōwa preferred to think of himself as an amateur naturalist, perhaps in the tradition of a Victorian gentleman.

After graduating from the Peers' School in 1914 Hirohito continued his studies until 1921 at the same kind of special institute, the Tōgū-gogakumonsho, which had been established for Yoshihito earlier. There, he was exposed to a broad curriculum devised primarily by the eminent Confucian scholar Sugiura Shigetake (Jūgō), whose interests also included agricultural science and chemistry, both of which he had studied in England. Under Sugiura's general guidance and that of the institute's director, Admiral Tōgō Heihachirō, Hirohito heard lectures by distinguished scholars on such subjects as Confucian ethics, Japanese and Chinese history, world history, law, French, mathematics, physics, chemistry, and geography. He also received instruction in military strategy and tactics and learned about his future role as commander-in-chief while serving as an officer in the army and navy. He was keenly interested in military affairs, and it is crucial to note that although he developed a strong aversion to war, Hirohito was by no means ever a convinced pacifist.

As one would expect, much emphasis was placed in Hirohito's education on the history and traditions of the imperial house. For instance, he studied the lives of great loyalist heroes like the medieval warrior Kusunoki Masashige, who fought for Emperor Go-Daigo against the Kamakura shogunate in the fourteenth century. Hirohito was also taught the Shintō legends and myths glorifying the imperial house. The historian Shiratori Kurakichi encouraged him to see the story of Japan's creation by the Sun Goddess and her offspring, and other such tales, not as actual historical events which could be verified on the basis of reliable evidence, but rather as invaluable parts of Japan's unique cultural heritage, which defined what it meant to be Japanese. Accordingly, although Emperor Shōwa never personally believed that he was a "manifest deity," he still dutifully performed the Shintō rites as was expected of him and always felt deeply responsible for preserving the imperial house.

What is more, like Motoda Eifu earlier, Sugiura in particular drew from the Confucian tradition in emphasizing to Hirohito the ideal of government based upon "imperial virtue." Sugiura taught that while political responsibility lay with the ministers of state, the emperor, as moral exemplar to the nation, was morally responsible for the nation's welfare. Years later, Prince Saionji would similarly advise Shōwa to emulate Emperor Meiji in setting a moral example for his subjects. During a palace tea party given in Saionji's honor in 1934, Saionji said that if Shōwa "wished to set an example for the people, he should say nothing at all but should simply do so as a matter of fact. With this kind of subtle attitude, [the Emperor] should strive to perfect his imperial virtue."[11] For Saionji, the ancient Chinese principle of political non-assertion (or *wu wei*, "non-action") on the part of a virtuous sovereign went hand in hand with the modern system of constitutional monarchy in which the emperor did not rule directly but only through his ministers of state.

These aspects of his Confucian training at the Tōgū-gogakumonsho remained important to Hirohito in later life. As we will see, after Japan's crushing defeat in 1945 he was determined to abdicate, assuming moral responsibility for war. More generally, from the beginning of his reign Hirohito reflected the idea (at least in abstract terms) that the government should always show "good faith" in providing for the people's welfare, which was implicit in Sugiura's lessons on "imperial virtue." The informative diary of his chief aide-de-camp in the early 1930s, General Honjō Shigeru, quotes Shōwa as saying on one occasion, "The Russian imperial government fell because the imperial court only worked for its own prosperity and neglected the welfare of the people." Shōwa then recited Confucius: "'When there is a shortage in the land, first abandon soldiers, then abandon food. But when it comes to the good faith of the state, it can never be abandoned.'" Shōwa commented to Honjō, "We must reflect seriously upon Confucius' teaching about the need for the state to act on good faith."[12]

Yet despite such sentiments it must be said that Shōwa's view of "the people" and of their welfare was very patrician, to put it mildly. Honjō recounts that Shōwa once told him during the Great Depression, when referring to the hard-pressed villagers, "It is of course necessary to sympathize with the dire plight of the peasants but peasants in their own way lead happy lives.... [They] should think about the pleasures of nature that are there for them to enjoy and not dwell on merely the unpleasant aspects of their lives."[13]

Hirohito's courses included the study of the natural world with Dr. Hattori Hirotaru, who introduced him to Darwin's theory of evolution and later assisted him in his biological research. It was during this period at the Tōgū-gogakumonsho that Hirohito's childhood interest in discovering and classifying specimens developed into a lifelong passion. If Taishō would have been happier as a military officer, Shōwa probably would have rather been a scientist (or a naturalist) than an emperor. As Kanroji states, "the only freedom Emperor Hirohito enjoys is when working with a microscope, absorbed in a factual world quite different from that normally inhabited by a crown prince or emperor."[14]

It was no accident that Shōwa's first rescript (which, unusually, he wrote himself) referred to "the process of evolution" and to "progress in view of this period of evolution." Under Hattori's influence, and like many other Japanese who had discovered Darwin's ideas, Hirohito took it for granted that there was a rational correspondence between the evolution of species through the "laws" of selective adaptation in the natural world and the historical evolution of human societies from primitivism toward "civilization." In this perception it followed that just as nature was comprised of mutually interdependent organisms, political and social institutions should function interdependently, each performing its allotted task, under the rule of law and for the benefit of all.[15]

The significance of this world view for Hirohito's subsequent political career was that in due course it would make him especially responsive to the apparent rationality of Minobe's "emperor-organ" theory, which, to reiterate, gained currency at court and in Japanese academic circles in the late Meiji and early Taishō periods. Minobe's constitutional interpretation—that the emperor was one organ (albeit the highest, and the source of legitimacy) of many interdependent "organs" of state, and that each organ had an assigned jurisdiction and responsibility—appealed to Hirohito's temperament as someone who appreciated the inherent order he discerned in nature as he "carefully checked and recorded" his specimens. This is probably why as emperor Hirohito would apply the "emperor-organ theory" so inflexibly to his own political conduct and with the same passion for playing by the "rules" of the constitution that he had displayed when playing games as a child.

Hirohito, needless to say, did not identify with Minobe's ideas all at once. Rather, he grew into them, like a suit of clothes, as subsequent experiences seemingly authenticated the force of Minobe's ideas. Here, his visit to England in 1921 was a watershed in Hirohito's political education.

At the time of his European tour, Hirohito was young and highly impressionable; every novelty aroused his interest. To illustrate, Colonel (later, Major-General) F. S. G. Piggott, who was assigned to escort the crown prince in England, was responsible for having him fitted out in a British military uniform for his visit to Aldershot. This involved trips to a tailor, a hatter, and a bootmaker. At the hatter's it was necessary to use a "conformature" to measure Hirohito's head. Piggott writes,

> I explained to the Prince that this strange-looking apparatus must be placed on his head. It intrigued him greatly, and we laughed together as he looked at himself in the glass; he saluted and assumed various other postures with the ingenious machine still on his brow…. [The visit was a] definite success.[16]

Given that Hirohito was so open to new experiences, it is not surprising that he was enthralled by King George V, who treated him warmly with a fatherly affection, as when the King, who was "only half-dressed, wearing trousers, braces, carpet slippers and an open shirt," came one morning to Hirohito's room to see if he had everything he needed for the day.[17]

They frequently talked about politics, including the King's position and role in the English political system. Shōwa recalled to newspaper reporters in 1961, "I had friendly conversations with King George V during my stay of three nights at Buckingham Palace and was able to gain a first-hand knowledge of English politics."[18]

Hirohito learned more in this regard from Professor J. R. Tanner, an expert on British constitutional history at St. John's College, Cambridge, who presented an hour-long lecture to Hirohito when he visited Cambridge to receive an honorary degree. In brief, Tanner emphasized that in the English system of constitutional monarchy, the people's rights are guaranteed while those of the monarch are limited. Whatever the personal wishes of the king (or queen) might be, the king's role is to reflect and symbolize the general will of the people, as determined by Parliament. The king, Tanner continued, may generally regulate domestic and foreign policy but only with the advice and consent of his ministers; the king has the right to be consulted, to encourage, and to warn, but he does not govern in his own right. In domestic and international affairs his primary function is to symbolize the unity of the nation and the greatness of the British empire.[19]

Despite the differences between the English and Japanese constitutions, Tanner's analysis of the English system sufficiently resembled Minobe's interpretation of the Meiji constitution to help make it authoritative to the founders of the regency, including Hirohito. For after he became regent in November 1921, if indeed not before, Hirohito saw himself as an "organ" of the state with limited powers—in effect as an English-style constitutional monarch. More than anyone else, it was Prince Saionji who strongly reinforced Hirohito's constitutional self-image, for Saionji perceived the monarchy in the same way. A proponent of the "emperor-organ theory" who invited Minobe to lecture from time to time at court, "Like Minobe, Saionji recognized no autonomous role for the Emperor and believed that constitutionally the Emperor could act only on the advice of his ministers and further that the quality of this advice should be subject to criticism."[20]

Until Saionji died in 1940 he advised Emperor Shōwa accordingly. This stance posed few risks for the court during the 1920s when, with the political parties in the ascendancy, there was a general resonance between the "emperor-organ theory" and an assertive "parliamentary ideology" which "situated the practice of parliamentary government at the center and imperial authority at the legitimating circumference, rather than the reverse," of the political order.[21] But in the 1930s, the political ascendancy of the military and the weakening of this "parliamentary ideology" meant that imperial authority would be restored to the political "center" and used to legitimize the growing power of the military. As this happened, the dilemma facing Shōwa would be whether to try and resist by asserting the emperor's constitutional prerogatives over the military—in which case he would risk subverting the principles of limited monarchy—or whether, as a constitutional monarch, he should sanction military priorities even though he disagreed with them, at the certain risk of playing right into the hands of the military.

Due to Saionji's influence and his own ingrained tendency to "absolutize" the principles of constitutional monarchy,[22] Shōwa chose the latter course. As Prince Konoe Fumimaro observed in 1945, when Japan stood in the ruins of a lost war:

> Out of reserve, the Emperor seldom expresses his own
> views. Prince Saionji and count Makino taught His
> Majesty not to take the initiative, in adherence to the
> British-style constitution, but the Japanese constitution
> exists on the premise of the Emperor's personal admin-
> istration. It is fundamentally different from the British
> constitution. Especially in regard to the matter of the
> supreme command, the government has no voice
> whatever. It is the Emperor alone who can control both
> the government and the supreme command.... If the
> emperor merely gives encouragement or advice as in
> England, military affairs and political diplomacy can-
> not advance in unison."[23]

To be sure, in some respects this passage is very mislead-
ing. We have already seen, as Konoe himself would have
known, that since Meiji's day the ambiguity of the constitution had made the emperor's "control" of the government and
supreme command at best a theoretical proposition. Furthermore, Konoe will emerge in the pages that follow as one of
many leading political and military figures who thwarted
even the possibility of Shōwa's assuming "control." However,
there is no doubt that by resolutely adhering to the principles
of limited monarchy, as if Japan were England, Shōwa and his
advisers neutralized the imperial court politically even as
other elites exploited the emperor's authority in committing
Japan to aggression and war in the period from 1926 to 1941.
It is to this story which we now turn.

●

●

The Palace and Political Crisis

After World War I Japan broadly subscribed to the spirit of internationalism which was advocated in the League of Nations. Similarly, at the Washington Conference (1921–22) Japan agreed to end the Anglo-Japanese Alliance in favor of signing a series of collective security treaties with the Western powers, which set limits on naval armament and recognized the sovereignty and territorial integrity of China. In 1925 Japan also extended diplomatic recognition to the Soviet Union, despite the Comintern's sponsorship of Communist movements in Asia. On other fronts, Japanese-American relations were troubled by American anti-Japanese immigration laws, which especially rankled the Japanese after the failure of the League to adopt Japan's proposed racial equality clause in its Covenant. Even so, there was little sign in the 1920s of the future crisis that would overtake Japanese-American relations. Japan's fundamental adherence to a policy of free trade through peaceful "cooperative diplomacy" mostly fell into line with America's "Open Door" policy, enunciated earlier by Secretary of State John Hay at the turn of the century.

Placing their trust in international agreements as the means of ensuring peace and stability in Asia, Hirohito, Saionji, Makino, and other leading constitutional monarchists at court all approved of the government's "cooperative diplomacy" towards the Anglo-American powers and China.[24] Events in China, however, soon disrupted this vision of a lasting Asian peace. To explain, Chiang Kai-shek's ultimately successful "northern expedition," begun in 1926 to unify China under Nationalist (Kuomintang) control, alarmed officers in the Kwantung Army stationed in South Manchuria. They feared that Japan's client in north China, the warlord Chang Tso-lin, would prove unreliable in helping to prevent Chiang from threatening Japan's treaty rights in South Manchuria. Accordingly, in June 1928 they murdered Chang by blowing up his train as it approached Mukden, blaming his death on "Chinese bandits." This "Chang Tso-lin Incident" presented Shōwa with the first of many crises, following in close succession.

At once the court pressed Prime Minister Tanaka Giichi to identify and punish Chang's killers. But Tanaka, frustrated by the army's refusal to cooperate, prevaricated for nearly a year, and Shōwa grew increasingly irritated, impatient to hold the army and the cabinet accountable under the rule of law. He and his advisers were also keen to avoid an international incident over Chang's murder. Only reluctantly, in June 1927 and again in the spring of 1928, had Shōwa sanctioned Tanaka's earlier policy of dispatching troops to protect Japanese nationals in Shantung from Chiang Kai-shek's advancing forces on the northern expedition.

Sensing that Shōwa was angry with Tanaka for failing to hold the army accountable for Chang Tso-lin's death, Saionji and Makino (who had become lord keeper of the privy seal in 1925) debated inconclusively during the spring and early summer of 1929 on how far a constitutional monarch should go in reprimanding a prime minister. Finally, after experts in constitutional law had advised that it would indeed be appropriate for Shōwa formally to admonish Tanaka, he summoned Tanaka to the palace on June 27 and questioned his handling of the Chang Tso-lin Incident. Many years later Shōwa remembered that Tanaka replied evasively: "Because what Tanaka told me differed from what he had said before, I spoke to him in a strong manner and said to him, is this not different from what you said before? How about submitting your resignation?"[25]

Shōwa, it seems, had meant this as a rhetorical question, to impress upon Tanaka his overall responsibility for getting the army to disclose the identity of Chang Tso-lin's killers. "When I asked should he not resign, this was a warning, not a 'veto,'" he explained. However, Tanaka's loyalist rhetoric (see last chapter) reflected a profound personal respect for the throne, and he interpreted Shōwa's question as a dismissal, resigning on July 2. It alarmed Shōwa to see that his intervention had caused the cabinet to fall, since that had not been his intention. Consequently, "Ever since this incident, whenever the cabinet reported to me, I decided to approve [its policies], even if I disagreed with them myself."[26]

Subsequently, Chang's assailants were subjected to military discipline, although in the circumstances their punishments were relatively light, and the "Chang Tso-lin Incident" was eclipsed by the impact of the Great Depression, following the crash of the stock market on Wall Street in New York. In 1930 and 1931 thousands of urban workers were left unemployed and many rural areas were left destitute by the collapse of American markets for Japanese exports, especially textiles, and by a precipitous fall in the price of silk and other agricultural products. These conditions soon provided fertile ground for political terrorism within Japan, and although by 1932 the economy was well on the way to recovery owing to the government's program of industrial rationalization, the erection of Western protectionist barriers prompted urgent Japanese calls for regional economic sufficiency in northeast Asia.

Early in the Depression, Emperor Shōwa was confronted by the second major test of his reign, the London Naval Treaty controversy of 1930. At stake in this crisis was whether, as the Navy Chief of Staff Admiral Katō Kanji claimed, the Minseitō cabinet of Prime Minister Hamaguchi Osachi (Yūkō) had violated the right of supreme command by agreeing to a naval arms limitation treaty which put the Japanese fleet at a disadvantage in comparison with the British and American navies. When Hamaguchi signed the treaty on April 22, Katō protested that under article XI of the constitution, matters pertaining to national security could only be decided by the army and navy general staff offices, not by the prime minister or the cabinet. He vigorously opposed Japan's ratification of the treaty on the same grounds.

Acting upon Saionji's advice, Shōwa refrained from any public involvement as Japan was torn by bitter disagreements over the treaty issue. However, he did exert informal imperial influence at court to assist the beleaguered Hamaguchi. Throughout, Shōwa believed, as Professor Minobe Tatsukichi had advised the court, that Hamaguchi had not violated the right of supreme command. Thus, when Katō tried to use his right of direct access to the throne to oppose the treaty in March and again in early April, he was rebuffed by the grand chamberlain, Admiral Suzuki Kantarō, which allowed Hamaguchi to see Shōwa first and obtain his sanction for the treaty. Later, on June 10, Katō finally managed to obtain an audience with Shōwa, but as he complained afterward, "I have just reported to the throne, but His Majesty had nothing at all to say...."[27] Frustrated, Katō resigned the next day. He was replaced by an admiral who agreed to treaty ratification.

The London Naval Treaty was formally ratified by the privy council on October 1, 1930. Unfortunately, however, this was scarcely the end of the matter. The fundamental question of who, or what agency, exercised the emperor's supreme command prerogative in determining national security requirements remained unsettled. On November 14 Hamaguchi was shot by a right-wing assailant and later died of his wounds. And finally, the London Naval Treaty itself lapsed in 1936, after Japan withdrew the previous year from a second London naval conference which was to have renewed the original treaty. The result was a naval arms race with Britain and America, which escalated dramatically later in the decade.

Within a year of Japan's ratification of the London Naval Treaty there erupted yet another, far more serious crisis—the Manchurian Incident, the first major war of Shōwa's reign. Although the Incident was brought to an end with the Tangku truce between Japan and China in May 1933, Japan had only narrowly avoided war with the Western powers when the Incident spread to Shanghai in early 1932, the Kwantung Army had created the puppet state of Manchukuo in September 1932, and Japan had withdrawn from the League of Nations in March 1933. Another serous casualty of the Incident within Japan itself was party government, which came to a violent end with the murder in May 1932 of Prime Minister Inukai Tsuyoshi (Ki), to be discussed shortly.

The Manchurian Incident began on the night of September 18, 1931, when a bomb exploded on the South Manchurian Railway line at Mukden. The Kwantung Army immediately blamed Chinese subversives, but in truth the explosion was set off by officers of the Kwantung Army general staff who were acting unilaterally without the approval of either their commander or the Tokyo government. They wanted to create a pretext for the seizure of all of Manchuria and to force the Tokyo government into a stronger foreign policy on behalf of Japan's strategic and economic interests in northeast Asia. This radical defiance by the military of civil authority directly challenged Shōwa's optimistic belief in the rule of law. He was therefore determined to ensure, as General Honjō Shigeru observed, "that the lines of authority for governance, supreme command, foreign affairs, and so on were clearly distinguished and that the agencies involved did not transgress the proper bounds of their areas of responsibility."[28] It will be recalled that Meiji had spoken in precisely the same terms during the Sino-Japanese War.

The possible international repercussions of the Incident were of no less concern to Shōwa. As Japanese army units quickly pushed out from Mukden, he remarked in consternation:

> I believe that international justice and good faith are important and I am striving to preserve world peace…. But the forces overseas do not heed my commands and are recklessly expanding the incident. [The incident] causes me no end of anguish. This could result in intervention by the major powers and the destruction of our nation and people…. When I think of all these problems I cannot sleep at night.[29]

Soon after he was informed of the hostilities in Manchuria, Shōwa told Prime Minister Wakatsuki Reijirō (Hamaguchi's successor), "The government's policy of non-enlargement is most proper. Strive to achieve that goal." He also ordered Army Chief of Staff General Kanaya Hanzō to restrain the Kwantung Army. However, when Japanese forces stationed in Korea also poured into Manchuria without authorization, it was clear that Kanaya was as powerless as Wakatsuki to stop the Incident. Following Wakatsuki's resignation in December 1931—by which time almost all of Manchuria had been occupied and Japanese troops were poised to invade Jehol Province next door—Shōwa declared to the new prime minister, Inukai Tsuyoshi, that "The indiscipline and violence of the military and their meddling in domestic and foreign affairs is something which, for the welfare of the nation, must be viewed with apprehension. Be mindful of my anxiety."[30]

Inukai also failed to limit the Incident, however, and in early 1932 the fighting spread to Shanghai. Fearing Western intervention against Japan, Shōwa ordered General Shirakawa Yoshinori to restore peace in Shanghai, which Shirakawa managed to do, although he himself was killed in April that year. Out of gratitude Shōwa later composed a poem in Shirakawa's honor, which was not made public until after World War II. Army leaders feared Shōwa's solicitude for peace would offend the troops who had been called upon to risk their lives at the front. And indeed, during the Manchurian Incident many in the armed forces regretted that while they were "fighting a sacred war in order to expand national power and prestige, the Emperor does not approve and the government is obstructing every move."[31] Another typical army complaint was that Shōwa was playing mah jong and indulging his research interests in marine biology while soldiers died on the Asian mainland.

Shōwa was very sensitive to these criticisms of his personal life. Even after the Manchurian Incident, he often asked Honjō if it would be appropriate for him to take a break and go collecting specimens in the sea off of Hayama. At one point in 1934, when Shōwa fell ill from mental and physical exhaustion, he was advised by his brother Chichibu to take a short vacation. Shōwa was afraid of what the military would think if he did this, but Honjō reassured him that it would be reasonable for him to go for a brief holiday, as long as army and navy leaders were told in advance that this was absolutely necessary for the sake of his health.[32]

The Manchurian Incident had been perpetrated by men who cynically professed their loyalty to Shōwa while defying his will for peace. The radical young officers who assassinated Inukai in the infamous "May 15, 1932 Incident" likewise began their manifesto by proclaiming, "In the name of the Emperor, destroy the evil advisers around the throne...." In these circumstances Shōwa could do little to roll back the Manchurian Incident. His orders for restraint were typically ignored by the army.

Casting about for a solution, Shōwa evidently felt that if the Kwantung Army could not be held in check, perhaps the crisis in Manchuria could at least be ended speedily if he sanctioned specific operations that might achieve this objective. A case in point was his authorization, on February 4, 1933, of the army's plan—which the cabinet had not approved—to invade Jehol. But then, seeing that this campaign would worsen

Japan's position in the League of Nations, where Japanese aggression in Manchuria had been roundly condemned, Shōwa changed his mind six days later, only to be told by the army chief of staff that since he had already sanctioned the campaign, it was too late to call it off.[33] In the event, Japanese forces seized Jehol and added it to the new "state" of Manchukuo.

When the government decided to withdraw from the League of Nations in March 1933, Shōwa duly sanctioned this step even though he personally regretted it and hoped that Japan might still find ways to cooperate with the League in the years ahead. In his rescript announcing Japan's exodus, he wanted to state very explicitly that henceforth there should be a strict separation of the civil and military branches of government, to ensure civil control of the military. But army authorities insisted on the bland statement, "We command that all public servants, whether civil or military, shall faithfully perform each his appointed duty." In every sense, then, the Manchurian Incident exposed the powerlessness of the imperial court to bring the military to heel.

Following the murders of Hamaguchi and Inukai, not to mention other, aborted instances of terrorism, Shōwa and his advisers were now preoccupied with the rising threat of fascism in Japan. This danger was mainly posed by young officers and right-wing civilian activists who advocated a "Shōwa Restoration" and the transfer of power to the military under the cloak of imperial rule. Shōwa therefore admonished Saionji to recommend a successor to Inukai who would oppose "fascism," uphold the constitution, and work for peace. Otherwise, he said, "I would not be able to justify and vindicate myself to [the spirit of] Emperor Meiji."[34] Saionji responded by recommending the relatively moderate Admiral Saitō Makoto, who formed the first of a long line of bureaucratic, non-party cabinets in prewar Japan.

The Honjō diary reveals that at one point during the Manchurian crisis Shōwa's brother, Prince Chichibu, advised that the only way to deal with the threat of fascism was for Shōwa to assume personal charge of the government even if it meant suspending the constitution. But Shōwa heatedly refused this course of action, arguing that not even the threat of fascism could possibly justify this radical a departure from his obligations as a constitutional monarch. He reportedly said later that, as Honjō relates it,

> he would never agree to anything that would besmirch the honor of his ancestors. There is some talk of establishing personal rule, but he was adhering to fundamental principles and overseeing political affairs according to the constitution.... What more could he do? Moreover, suspension of the constitution means destroying what Emperor Meiji had created. This, he asserted, could never be allowed to happen.[35]

Saionji readily agreed. He and Makino thus endeavored to maintain Shōwa "above the clouds" of political conflict. They did not share Prince Konoe Fumimaro's belief that "The Emperor, holding very liberal ideas, may be the main cause of friction with the army." But thinking it would be easier to restrain Shōwa than the army, it was "agreed that the Emperor had better not say anything further unless necessary."[36] Saionji also cautioned, "It is not necessary to lie but tell the Emperor things that will please him in order to ease his mind."[37]

Shōwa's mind was hardly eased, however, when in January 1932 a Korean nationalist tried to kill him by throwing a bomb at his passing car. Shōwa was unharmed but it is noteworthy that Kinoshita Michio, an official in the imperial household ministry, suggested that the court might exploit this incident to strengthen public sympathy with the emperor and have Shōwa issue a statement to the effect that such signs of radical dissent were partly due to the emperor's own lack of virtue.[38] Nothing came of the proposal, yet it indicates the extent to which the notion of "imperial virtue" as a normative ideal still held sway at court.

Outwardly, Shōwa himself maintained the appearance of calm in these turbulent years. He seemed quite unruffled to the American Ambassador Joseph Grew, who recalled after their first meeting, in June 1932, that "The Emperor Hirohito is young—thirty-one, I believe; he has a small mustache and glasses and smiles pleasantly when talking." Similarly, at a party in February 1934 to celebrate the birth of Prince Akihito on December 21 the previous year, Hirohito surprised Grew by asking casually, "How's Sambo?"—the Grews' dog which had recently been rescued after falling into the imperial palace moat.[39]

Yet beneath Shōwa's apparent composure, he was personally unnerved by the general atmosphere of violence that now prevailed in Japan. Heightened security also unsettled him. Hemmed in by policemen who were deployed everywhere around the palace, and constrained by his advisers, he often complained bitterly, "I cannot go anywhere." Like Taishō

earlier, he increasingly found release from the strains of office
by playing with his children, but any images of Shōwa as a
family man never reached the public. In 1936, for example,
the imperial household ministry censored a photograph showing him dressed in a suit as he relaxed with the members of his
family. Only photographs depicting him unsmiling and in
military uniform were judged suitable for a "manifest deity"
and leader of the armed forces.

Thus, the people, who had been whipped into a patriotic
frenzy during the Manchurian Incident, never knew that at
court Shōwa had opposed Japan's seizure of Manchuria. Nor
did his subjects know that Shōwa privately defended Professor Minobe Tatsukichi in 1935, when Minobe and his "emperor-organ" theory were widely and vociferously attacked by
conservative ultranationalists in the Diet and in the Imperial
Reservists' Association, who mounted a movement "to clarify
the national polity." In the crisis atmosphere of the 1930s his
opponents found intolerable Minobe's contention that the emperor was a mere "organ" of the state and not an absolute god-
king who personified the imperial state. They considered
Minobe a traitor.

Shōwa fervently rejected this view of Minobe. He asserted,
"I think Minobe is not at all disloyal. Is there really anyone his
equal in Japan today? To bury such a scholar would be lam-
entable."[40] During innumerable discussions with his chief
aide-de-camp, Shōwa stood by Minobe. Denying that he or
any emperor was a god, as Minobe's critics insisted, Shōwa
said of such beliefs (as Honjō paraphrases him): "if matters of
faith and belief were used to suppress scientific theories, then
world progress would be hindered. Theories such as evolution

would have to be overturned." The idea that he ruled as a god rather than reigned as a constitutional monarch represented nothing less than the "bane of despotism."[41] Shōwa would often use this phrase to express his great anxiety that Japan might someday abandon Meiji's legacy of constitutional government.

His reasoning was never made public, for fear of violent right-wing reprisals. A member of the court circle later put it this way: "in politics, it is the wish of the Emperor to respect and guard strictly the spirit of the constitution, but this cannot be told to the people…. The Emperor's ideas are not at all evident either in politics or diplomacy." Here, the problem was: "If one should explain that it is the Emperor's desire to conduct a completely constitutional government, it is said that Saionji, Makino, or other immediate officials do what they please behind the scenes by using the name of the Emperor."[42]

Thus, by the time the "Minobe Incident" died down in late 1935, Minobe and his interpretation of the constitution were thoroughly discredited and the fiction that a divine emperor ruled as well as reigned was now completely sacrosanct, at least in the patriotic rhetoric of Japanese ultranationalism. What made this fiction of imperial absolutism especially dangerous was that the military might use it, after seizing control of the emperor, to legitimize their power by invoking his authority. This in fact nearly happened in the most dramatic domestic crisis of Shōwa's reign: the army rebellion of February 1936.

Early in the snowy morning of the 26th, 1,400 soldiers allied with the army's "imperial way" faction (Kōdō-ha) seized control of central Tokyo, expecting the emperor to proclaim a "Shōwa Restoration" regime under the leadership of an imperial way general. With "revere the emperor, destroy the traitors" as their slogan, designated hit squads murdered the finance minister, the lord keeper of the privy seal (former prime minister Saitō Makoto), and a leading general in the rival "control faction" (*Tōsei-ha*). They also tried to kill the prime minister, Admiral Okada Keisuke (who had followed Saitō in office), but he managed to escape.

When first informed of the rebellion, Shōwa reportedly said, "It's all due to a failing in me."[43] Whether he meant by this a failure of moral leadership on his part, or more probably a failure to anticipate the crisis, is unknown. But in any case, he acted with uncharacteristic boldness, commanding the army minister: "I will give you exactly one hour to suppress the rebels." Later, he vowed that if necessary he would personally lead loyalist units against the rebels, and referring to the assassinations he declared, "How can we not condemn the spirit of these criminally brutal officers who killed my aged subjects, who were my hands and feet...?"[44]

However, the crisis passed almost as quickly as it had arisen. Spurred by Emperor Shōwa and by control faction leaders who were determined to crush the imperial way faction, the army faced down the rebels, supported by the navy and its amassing warships in Tokyo Bay. After three days of turmoil, they surrendered on the 29th. Greatly relieved, Shōwa at once resolved to purge the army:

Their actions have violated the constitution, gone against Emperor Meiji's Rescript to Soldiers and Sailors, blackened the national polity, and defiled its purity. The army should now be cleansed thoroughly ... steps should be taken to prevent such a disgraceful incident from ever happening again.[45]

Unfortunately, the process of cleansing the army did not get very far because Shōwa, succumbing to indecision, soon backed away out of fear that any purges might provoke further unrest in the armed forces. With major elements of the imperial way faction still intact, and with the government dependent upon the control faction to preserve order in the army, this left the problem of army factionalism unresolved.

Still, Japan's system of constitutional government had survived this unprecedented crisis, which was what mattered the most to Shōwa at the time. Later recalling his role in quelling the rebellion, he even regretted that "As a constitutional monarch I overstepped my authority; I should have asked the cabinet to order their suppression."[46] Looking ahead, his intervention in 1936 to preserve constitutional government did not mean that he was similarly prepared to intervene on behalf of peace when the government decided on war. As Shōwa saw it, to try and overturn foreign policy decisions legally taken by the government was a completely different proposition and one that he deliberately rejected because it conflicted with his self-image as a constitutional monarch. He believed that if he should fail to sanction war decisions, even when he personally opposed them, he would only sabotage the very constitutional system he had always pledged to uphold. It was for this reason, and because of anxieties of what might otherwise happen to him, that he quickly reverted to being an emperor "above the clouds" when Japan was buffeted by the winds of war.

Shōwa's Road to Pearl Harbor

The Manchurian Incident left Japan in a position to extend its political and economic influence in north China with a view to incorporating the region into a self-sufficient "Yen bloc," which also included Japan and Manchukuo. War with China had not been part of this overall plan. The Japanese units that became involved in hostilities with Chinese forces at Marco Polo Bridge near Peking on the night of July 7, 1937, were carrying out exercises in preparation for a possible war with the Soviet Union, not China.

However, this "Marco Polo Bridge Incident" soon flared into the "China Incident," Japan's undeclared war on China, which lasted until Japan surrendered to the Allies in 1945. According to some estimates, the "China Incident" cost the lives of more than three million Chinese soldiers and left nearly six million Chinese civilians dead or injured; 447,000 Japanese military personnel are thought to have died in the conflict, with thousands more wounded or sick. The Incident also witnessed some of the worst wartime Japanese atrocities: the well-known "rape of Nanking" in December 1937—in which Japanese troops ran amok, killing and torturing perhaps as many as 200,000 Chinese soldiers and civilians who were trapped there—and the cruel lethal experiments in biological warfare conducted by Unit 731 of the imperial army on Chinese and Russians in Manchuria, not to mention similar experiments in China south of the Great Wall.

From its inception, the China Incident was very controversial within Japanese ruling circles, including the army. Army Minister Sugiyama Hajime (Gen) and key commanders in the field supported the war, arguing that Japan's national security was at stake in China. However, both Army Chief of Staff Prince Kan'in Kotohito (Shōwa's cousin) and Vice-Chief General Tada Shun preferred a negotiated settlement with China. They thought that Russia, not China, was a more important foe because of the recent buildup of Soviet troops along the Manchukuo border. As for Prime Minister Konoe Fumimaro, who had assumed power in June 1937, he at first opposed the war but then changed to a belligerent position. His turnabout is difficult to explain. Ironically, it is possible that Konoe escalated the war as a means of asserting his political control over the military.[47] If this was his goal, Konoe was only fooling himself.

To reconcile these divisions, in November 1937 it was decided to establish the mechanism of the liaison conference (*renraku kaigi*), consisting of the prime minister and other leading cabinet members, including the army and navy ministers, and the army and navy chiefs of staff and their senior advisers. As "liaison conference" implies, the purpose was to promote decisions based on the broadest possible consensus, with the expectation that Shōwa, who never attended liaison conference meetings, would automatically ratify these decisions with the formal imperial will at ensuing imperial conferences (*gozen kaigi*; e.g., the members of the liaison conference plus the emperor and president of the privy council). This structure of decision-making, involving liaison and imperial conferences, would continue through World War II, albeit in a somewhat modified form.

Such were the circumstances when Emperor Shōwa arrived at a crucial juncture in his political career on January 14, 1938, the day he effectively sealed Japan's attempted conquest of China. It must be emphasized that early in the China Incident he had opposed war with China, although he seems to have been more concerned about the prospect of Western intervention on China's side than with the fate of China itself. As late as January 10, 1938, he had backed the demand of the army and navy chiefs of staff for an imperial conference at which the chiefs hoped to oppose Konoe's growing advocacy of all-out war with China. Konoe had agreed to an imperial conference, but seeing that Shōwa might speak out against the war, Konoe told Shōwa beforehand that it would be improper for him to say anything at this meeting. Accordingly, Shōwa remained silent when the imperial conference, which was held on the 11th, decided to endorse Konoe's policy of a "war of annihilation" against Nationalist China. General Tada later complained, "His Majesty said nothing. This is indeed just like the emperor-organ theory. From now on I want things to be decided by the imperial judgment."[48] Tada plainly hoped Shōwa would decisively intervene to restore peace in China.

The liaison conference met again on the 14th, to reconfirm and plan the implementation of this decision. During a recess in these especially acrimonious proceedings, Prince Kan'in sought an urgent audience with Shōwa at the palace in a final, desperate bid to enlist Shōwa's support for reversing Konoe's policy of crushing the Chiang Kai-shek regime. However, as Shōwa subsequently explained to Konoe, "I judged that this might surely be a plan to overturn what had already been determined [by the government] and I refused to see him."[49]

Tada had thus read Shōwa's intentions very accurately: in refusing to question the government's decision for war in China, despite his own desire for peace, Shōwa again revealed

•

161

•

his firm determination to act as an "organ" of state, in accordance with Minobe's now discredited theory. For Shōwa, the "bane of despotism" inherent in any imperial intervention was worse than the spectre of war itself. Admittedly, given that Konoe had already succeeded in forging a general political consensus for all-out war in China, it is probably unlikely that Shōwa could have reversed this decision even had he intervened decisively, as Kan'in and Tada had wished. Yet supported by the general staff office, a sufficiently forceful imperial intervention might just have avoided the rapid escalation of the China Incident in 1938, and in retrospect the appalling human costs of the China Incident would have made this a risk worth taking. As it happened, by mandating Konoe's policy of all-out war, Shōwa made the China Incident into a war of his own.

Britain and the United States did not directly intervene militarily on China's behalf, although they condemned Japan's aggression in China and provided material assistance to the Nationalists. Japan, however, simply could not conquer China. Japanese forces took control of the coastal provinces and inland transportation networks but not the vast rural hinterland. From his wartime capital at Chungking, Chiang Kaishek maintained a fierce Nationalist resistance, as did Mao Tse-tung's Communist army operating out of Yenan, Mao's seat of power in the north. Discouraged by this stalemate, Konoe resigned in January 1939.

Besides the China Incident, in 1938 and 1939 it looked as if Japan might also plunge into full-scale war with Russia. In July 1938, Shōwa was startled by the news that the Kwantung Army had engaged Russian forces in unauthorized hostilities at Changkufeng, on the disputed frontier between Korea, Manchukuo, and the Soviet Union. He angrily reprimanded Army Chief Kan'in and Army Minister Itagaki Seishirō[50] when they sought his sanction for military operations there. Shōwa declared, "The methods of the army in the past have been unpardonable. In the Manchuria incident and also in the doings at Marco Polo Bridge ... there was complete disobedience to central orders." Denouncing officers who in previous crises had blatantly usurped the right of supreme command as "arbitrary," "sneaky," and "altogether improper as my army," he continued, with rising impatience: "This is disgraceful. Nothing like that must happen this time.... You may not move one soldier [at Changkufeng] without my command."[51] However, any inference that he would actually assume command was purely rhetorical, and in any case his orders were again ignored. As would happen in similar hostilities at Nomonhan (on the border between Manchukuo and Outer Mongolia) the following year, the fighting at Changkufeng was ended only after heavy defeats inflicted by Russia.

Some members of Shōwa's entourage persisted in believing that, because of his continuing criticism of the military, Emperor Shōwa was the problem, not the army. This opinion was typified by Kido Kōichi, for one. In his capacity as lord keeper of the privy seal, Kido would become Shōwa's principal political adviser following Saionji's death on November 24, 1940. In 1939 he confided to another palace official:

The present Emperor is a scientist and very much a liberal as well as a man of peace. Therefore, if the Emperor's ideas are not changed to some extent, the great gap between His Majesty and the rightist groups will grow.... In order to lead the army, but still make it appear as if we were being led by them, we must also make it seem as if we understood the army a little better.[52]

However, Shōwa would not abandon his contempt for the army as long as the army kept going its own way, and the idea that the court could somehow "lead the army" bordered on pure fantasy. The Japanese military never seized power through a coup d'etat, but military priorities increasingly predominated in the short-lived bureaucratic cabinets that came and went following Konoe's resignation in 1939. The consequence was a military hegemony within the existing constitutional framework. During this period Japanese society was extensively militarized in the process of building a so-called "national defense state" (*kokubō kokka*). The government's "spiritual mobilization" campaigns, which aimed to foster public support for the war in China, were one facet of this process. Another was the national mobilization law, enacted in 1938, which in theory at least empowered the government to place the economy on a total war footing. Finally, a "New Structure Movement" (*shintaisei undō*) gave rise in October 1940 to the Imperial Rule Assistance Association (IRAA). This new political front, headed by Prime Minister Konoe after he returned to power in July that year, absorbed all existing parties, although it fell short of the kind of totalitarian controls seen in contemporary Germany.

What gave the military decisive leverage in Japanese foreign policy–making was the war in Europe, beginning with Germany's invasion of Poland in September 1939. After Germany rapidly conquered France, Belgium, and the Netherlands by the end of June 1940, there arose in Japan opportunistic demands for an alliance with Germany, lest Japan miss an unprecedented chance to create the so-called "Greater East Asia Co-Prosperity Sphere." Proponents of this new policy predicted that Britain would soon fall to German power in Europe. They argued that by deterring Russia to the north and the United States, an alliance with Germany would enable Japan to advance south, where the newly vulnerable Western colonies in Southeast Asia prompted Japanese visions of acquiring valuable natural resources and strategic military bases from which to strike at Chungking in the interior of China.

This overall policy of "defend the north, advance south" ultimately came to fruition during the tenure of Prince Konoe's second cabinet, which he formed on July 22, 1940. Under intense pressure from the army and pro-German "revisionist bureaucrats," Konoe and Foreign Minister Matsuoka Yōsuke led Japan into the Axis Alliance with Germany and Italy on September 27, 1940. On the preceding day Japan intimidated the French colonial authorities in Hanoi into permitting the stationing of Japanese forces in northern Indo-China. In April 1941, Japan went on to conclude a neutrality pact with the Soviet Union, further to secure the north, and in late July 1941 Japanese forces occupied southern as well as northern Indo-China. This last provocation immediately persuaded the United States to freeze Japanese assets in the U.S. (on July 25) and to place an embargo on oil exports to Japan (on August 1). America and Japan were now on a collision course.

To Emperor Shōwa, the decisions taken by the liaison conference to ally with Germany and advance south—which conference, to reiterate, Shōwa did not attend—were exceedingly dangerous because they greatly heightened the risk of war with the Anglo-American powers. While those policy options were being debated, he accordingly took every opportunity to warn government leaders, when he received them in audience at the palace, that they must not jeopardize the future of the empire in this way. For example, at an early stage in discussions concerning an alliance with Germany, he told a palace official that if Army Chief of Staff Kan'in, "ever mentions anything about participation in war [on Germany's side], I will definitely oppose it." He also used the emperor's customary right to pose "imperial questions" (*gokamon*) to warn Kan'in's successor, General Sugiyama, that the whole southern advance was fraught with peril. Sugiyama noted, on one occasion: "His Majesty's questions today indicated that he is filled with a desire to avoid recourse to force no matter what. I plan to use whatever opportunity that may arise to change his thinking on this question."[53]

Nevertheless, when presented with liaison conference decisions, Shōwa always formally ratified them in the imperial conferences which invariably followed, whatever his private reservations. Of the Axis Alliance, he later said, "Ultimately, I agreed with [the alliance] but this does not mean I was satisfied with it…. I believed Matsuoka that it would deter the United States."[54] Fortunately, when Germany called upon Japan to support "Operation Barbarossa"—Germany's invasion of Russia, begun in June 1941—the government refrained. Japan stayed out of war with Russia until the Soviet

Union invaded Manchuria after declaring war on Japan on August 8, 1945.

With the American embargo of oil to Japan now in place, the issue of war hovered darkly over negotiations in Washington between Japan and the United States from early August 1941. Should Japan submit to American demands that it withdraw from China, abandon the southern advance, and repudiate the Axis Alliance? Or should Japan go to war with the United States and Britain, to preserve the sovereign autonomy of the empire? This was the dilemma facing Japan's leaders, including Shōwa, as they viewed the present crisis. By far the majority, civilian and military alike, preferred the unknown risk of total war to the seemingly certain humiliation of a submissive peace. The real question therefore was war, how soon? Navy Chief of Staff Admiral Nagano Osami told Shōwa at the beginning of August, "it would be best if we act sooner than later because supplies [of oil] are dwindling day by day."[55]

Shōwa shared the navy's anxiety over oil but he worried that the navy was not adequately prepared for what would be the biggest war in Japanese history. The army struck him as equally unrealistic. During an audience on September 5 with both chiefs of staff, Sugiyama predicted it would take three months for Japan to control the southern Pacific. Shōwa sharply reminded Sugiyama that he had once said it would take three months to control China, which, although vast, was a much smaller area than the Pacific, but the China Incident was still raging on.[56]

The chiefs' failure to assure Shōwa that Japan could prevail was all the more ominous because two days earlier the liaison conference had decided that Japan should go to war with America by the end of October, if by then there was no prospect of an accommodation with the United States in the Washington talks. Thus, when the imperial conference met on September 6 to ratify this decision, Shōwa saw fit to depart from his usual silence on such occasions by reading a poem that Meiji had composed on the eve of the Russo-Japanese War:

All the seas, in every quarter,
Are as brothers to one another.
Why, then, do the winds and waves of strife
rage so turbulently throughout the world?

He meant to warn the government that diplomacy should be given a chance, but this very indirect expression of his desire for peace had no effect whatsoever. As the conference ended, a time bomb now ticked loudly in Japanese foreign policy.

It was defused, though, when Konoe and his cabinet suddenly resigned in mid-October, to avoid responsibility for taking Japan into total war. Through Lord Keeper of the Privy Seal Kido, Shōwa made it clear to Konoe's successor, Prime Minister Tōjō Hideki—whom Kido had recommended as the only man who could restrain the army—that he should give the Washington talks another chance without any deadline. Initially, Tōjō complied with this, but as Japan's stocks of oil fell by the day, the liaison conference decided on November 2, at the end of a very strained seventeen-hour meeting, that Japan should go to war in early December unless America accepted Japan's "New Order" in Asia and agreed to resume oil exports. A time-bomb again ticked in Japanese diplomacy.

Shōwa formally sanctioned this new deadline at an imperial conference three days later, this time without warning the government of the likely catastrophe war would bring. Then, on November 26, the government received the so-called "Hull note" from American Secretary of State Cordell Hull. This message was not intended to be an ultimatum. But by holding out little hope that the United States would soften its tough line, the note persuaded the Japanese government that war was now inevitable. Thus, when the new deadline passed without a breakthrough in Washington, Shōwa ratified the war decision at an imperial conference held on December 1, again without saying a word, and on December 7 (U.S. time) the navy executed its daring attack on the Amercian Pacific fleet based at Pearl Harbor. Because the encoded text of Japan's final note to the United States arrived late in Washington, and because Japanese Embassy officials had difficulty typing up a formal copy in English, it was not delivered to the American government until one hour after the attack had begun. This lack of Japan's "good faith" angered and dismayed Shōwa.[57]

However, there is no doubt that by November 1941, together with all of Japan's leaders, Shōwa had come fatalistically to believe that the country had no choice but to wage war. To repeat, Emperor Shōwa was no pacifist but rather, like everyone else in the government, a nationalist who was not prepared to see the empire reduced by American sanctions. Mindful of previous terrorist incidents, he was likewise convinced that "If at the time I had suppressed the advocacy of war, public opinion would have questioned why Japan,

EMPERORS OF THE RISING SUN

possessing a powerful army and navy, should submit to the
United States and I felt that a [pro-war] coup might occur."

In recalling his thinking at the time, another, more fundamental, consideration was that "As a constitutional monarch
in a constitutional political system, I had no choice but to sanction the decision by the Tōjō cabinet to begin the war"; "If I
were to have sanctioned it because I personally liked it, or if I
had not sanctioned it because I personally disliked it, I would
have been no different from a tyrant." He allowed that had he
been able to foresee the complete destruction of the empire, he
might have intervened against war. But the government's
final consensus for war would have made that a futile gesture,
and "There would have been a great rebellion within the
country, the men whom I trusted around me would have been
killed, and my own life would not have been guaranteed."[58]

Whether there would have been a "great rebellion" is perhaps problematical, but at every stage on the road to Pearl
Harbor Shōwa had continued to emulate his grandfather,
partly out of admiration for Meiji's strength of character in
comparison with Taishō, and more especially because Meiji
had embraced the same commitment to the principles of limited monarchy which Shōwa had vowed to uphold. Shōwa's
tragedy, if there was a tragic dimension to his career, was that
although he himself had opposed war—at least until November 1941—he absolutized those principles to the point where
he ruled out the kind of dramatic imperial intervention which
might have caused the government to think twice before
plunging into the maelstrom of total war. Although he did not
participate in liaison conference decisions for war, by sanctioning them he bore a significant share of legal and moral re-

sponsibility for the Asia-Pacific War, as well as for the China Incident.

Suyama Yukio has speculated that had Meiji, not Shōwa, been on the throne in this period, Meiji would have stood up to the military, and the China Incident and World War II in Asia and the Pacific would have been prevented. Supporting the view that Hirohito was a "mediocre" emperor, Suyama unequivocally rejects Saionji's higher esteem for Shōwa, as when Saionji once declared, "I served three emperors, Emperor Meiji, Emperor Taishō, and the present Emperor [Shōwa], but the best of them is Shōwa."[59]

Would Meiji have pursued a different course? He was a more forceful man than Shōwa, and he might not have carried his constitutional self-constraints to the same extremes. It is therefore conceivable that if faced with the same hard political choices that Shōwa faced, Meiji would have asserted himself more boldly in attempts to prevent war. Yet, it is also significant that Meiji ultimately suppressed his private reservations and sanctioned the government's decisions for war against China in 1894 and Russia in 1904. This makes it likely that he, no less than Shōwa, would have sanctioned decisions for war in the early Shōwa period, believing this was required of him as a constitutional monarch to hold the government intact under extreme pressure. If so, Meiji, too, would be remembered today for his share of war-responsibility in modern Japanese history.

World War and the Fall of the Japanese Empire

Once Japan was at war Shōwa naturally wanted Japan to prevail. He was thus very pleased that the Pearl Harbor attack had seriously crippled the American Pacific fleet, and in early March 1942 he was no less delighted with Japan's swift conquests, by then, of Hong Kong, Manila, Singapore, Batavia, and Rangoon. At the same time, referring to the problem of supplying Japanese forces in far-flung theaters of combat, he worried, "The results of the war are perhaps coming too quickly."[60] Similarly, throughout the war Shōwa frequently admonished the army and navy chiefs to improve operational cooperation between the services, which was badly deficient, and to cease their constant political squabbling over the allocation of aircraft. When informed of critical Japanese defeats, such as in the Battle of Midway (June 1942), he stoically showed little outward emotion when urging Japan's military elites to do their best in the future.

Encouraging the nation's morale was Shōwa's main wartime function, whether by reviewing the troops as he sat astride his white horse, or by opening the sessions of the imperial Diet with stirring rescripts prepared by the government, which exhorted the Japanese people to work hard for victory. These activities gave the impression that as commander-in-chief he was personally directing the war. But while he routinely read daily battle reports and approved military operations in a map room at the palace, for the most part Shōwa was no more in charge of the war than Meiji had been during the major wars of his reign. Furthermore, if to his subjects Shōwa appeared to be a warrior-king, in reality he wanted an early peace. He made this wish clear to Tōjō in February 1942: "I assume you have given full consideration to not losing any opportunity of ending the conflict. It is undesirable to have it prolonged in vain, for the sake of human peace." He added, "I

fear that the quality of our troops will decline if the war is prolonged."[61]

Tōjō, however, was committed to continuing the war, and
ironically, even after the tide of war had gone against Japan,
Shōwa himself helped to prolong the war in two significant
respects. Firstly, despite the early emergence of a secret "peace
faction" of former prime ministers, court officials, and indeed
several members of the imperial family, for a long while
Shōwa resisted their intrigues to oust Tōjō as a first step in
ending the war. In a word, he believed that Tōjō was indispensable to prosecuting the war until Japan was in a strong
enough position to negotiate for peace on favorable terms. In
November 1943 he argued about this with his younger
brother, Prince Takamatsu, declaring, "It is said that Tōjō is
no good, but who would be better? If there is no one better, is
there no alternative but to cooperate with the Tōjō cabinet?"[62]

For some in the anti-Tōjō camp Shōwa's stubborn defense
of Tōjō was sufficient to justify a radical step that would have
been inconceivable before the war. They privately agreed on
July 8, 1944, that Shōwa "should abdicate, the Crown Prince
[Akihito, then aged eleven] should succeed him, and Prince
Takamatsu should be appointed Regent." Their choice to replace Tōjō was Prince Higashikuni Naruhiko, who was to
strive for peace.[63] The loss of Saipan the preceding day, which
put Japanese cities within striking distance of American
bombers flying from the Marianas, further reinforced the
plotters' sense of urgency. However, removing Shōwa proved
unnecessary, for he too saw, albeit reluctantly, that Tōjō had
become a political liability. On July 13, he ordered Tōjō to
strengthen the supreme command, implying strongly this

could only be accomplished if Tōjō resigned. Tōjō complied the next day.

Secondly, Shōwa and Lord Keeper of the Privy Seal Kido failed to issue clear instructions to Tōjō's successor, General Koiso Kuniaki, that he was to work for peace, as the peace faction had expected. Shōwa evidently still agreed with military hardliners that Japan should wait for victory in a decisive battle before entering into peace negotiations. It was with this goal in mind that in 1945 he sanctioned Japanese operations in the battle of the Philippines, in which kamikaze suicide planes were used for the first time, and in the battle of Okinawa.[64] The results were catastrophic for Japan, which was isolated in the war following Germany's surrender and the end of the European war in May: by the end of June 1945, both the Philippines and Okinawa had fallen to the Allies. Moreover, Allied planes now bombed Japanese cities day and night at will.

Shōwa must have appreciated that all was lost long before this, as he toured the rubble of Tokyo after most of the city was decimated on March 9–10, 1945 by massive fire-bombing which killed an estimated 90,000 of his subjects. The burning down of the main part of the imperial palace itself, in an air raid on May 25, likewise symbolized Japan's extreme vulnerability to total destruction. Forced to take refuge with Empress Nagako in an underground bomb shelter near the imperial library, he reportedly exclaimed, "The main hall has caught fire! The main hall! There is so much there that was precious to the Meiji Emperor, so many irreplaceable things. I want that fire put out whatever it takes."[65] But the hall could not be saved and Meiji Shrine was burned down, too, that same day.

•

•

When it was proposed that he flee Tokyo, Shōwa refused, believing this would kindle a defeatist attitude among the people, which many of Japan's leaders now feared. In a meeting at the palace on February 14, Prince Konoe had warned him that unless Japan ended the war very soon, the monarchy would surely be threatened by Communist revolution, bred of war-weariness and the general breakdown of society. To Shōwa this was indeed a foreboding scenario. Yet Konoe had also predicted, in hindsight accurately, that "Even if we surrender unconditionally, I feel that in America's case she would not go so far as to reform Japan's *kokutai* [national polity] or abolish the imperial house."[66]

Shōwa concurred with Konoe's positive assessment of the Americans. He therefore urged the government to accept the Allies' Potsdam Proclamation, which was issued on July 26, and called for Japan's unconditional surrender; "I thought the Japanese race would be destroyed.... I thought we had to make peace even if I had to sacrifice my own life."[67] However, taking his cue from the military, Prime Minister Suzuki Kantarō, the former grand chamberlain who had succeeded Koiso in April, greeted the Proclamation with deliberate silence. This reconfirmed the decision of the United States to bludgeon Japan into submission, hence the atomic bombing of Hiroshima on August 6 and of Nagasaki on August 8. Both cities were obliterated with great loss of life and many of the survivors suffered horrible disfigurement, not to mention the insidious effects of radiation poisoning.

Years later, in December 1988, Nagasaki's Mayor Motoshima Hitoshi publicly blamed Shōwa, who was then seriously ill and soon to die, for not ending the war sooner than he did, before the atomic bombs were dropped. Shōwa bore a major share of responsibility for the war, Motoshima said. For this criticism, Motoshima was shot and wounded two years later by a right-wing extremist. Yet while Motoshima's views are certainly understandable, in August 1945 neither Shōwa nor anyone else in Japan knew the atomic bombs existed, much less their awesome destructive power; had he known this, Shōwa might have intervened sooner to ensure Japan's acceptance of the Potsdam terms of surrender.

The fact is, moreover, that even after the unprecedented use of these weapons, and despite Russia's sudden declaration of war on August 8, the supreme council for the direction of the war (which had superseded the liaison conference) remained deadlocked, as it had been for several months now, over the question of whether to surrender. Foreign Minister Tōgō Shigenori and most civilian leaders advocated immediate surrender. But the military still advocated war until the Allies guaranteed the future of the monarchy and made other concessions: that they would not occupy Japan, that Japan should be entrusted to carry out the war crimes trials foreshadowed in the Potsdam Proclamation, and so on.

It was at this point of complete impasse that Suzuki and Kido arranged for Shōwa to intervene on behalf of surrender, which by then he was most anxious to do. But it took two imperial interventions to end the war. The first occurred at an imperial conference convened late at night on August 9 in the emperor's bunker. Rising to his feet and visibly nervous, Shōwa stated, "I have given serious thought to the situation prevailing at home and abroad and have concluded that continuing the war can only mean destruction for the nation and

•
176
•

a prolongation of bloodshed and cruelty in the world." Using words Meiji had used earlier, he said:

> the time has come when we must bear the unbearable. When I recall the feelings of my Grandsire, the Emperor Meiji, at the time of the Triple Intervention, I swallow my own tears and give my sanction to the proposal to accept the Allied Proclamation on the basis outlined by the Foreign Minister.[68]

Shōwa's dramatic intervention spurred the participants to honor his will for peace, but only after seeking American assurances the next day that the imperial institution would be preserved. When the American government replied ambiguously that it would be up to "the freely expressed will of the Japanese people" to determine Japan's "ultimate form of government," the military again threw the supreme council into confusion by arguing that the future of the monarchy was still in jeopardy and hence the war had to be fought to the bitter end.

Thus, after more inconclusive debate, Shōwa intervened a second time, on the morning of August 14. He told the members of the supreme council, who had assembled again in the bomb shelter, "I have listened carefully to each of the arguments ... but my own thoughts have not undergone any change.... In short, I consider the [American] reply to be acceptable." "It is my desire," he continued, "that you, my Ministers of State, accede to my wishes and forthwith accept the Allied reply. In order that the people may know of my decision, I request you to prepare at once an Imperial Rescript so that I may broadcast to the nation." [69]

Shōwa recorded the rescript later that day, at the imperial household ministry building, located on the palace grounds. However, early on August 15, the day of the broadcast, die-hard soldiers attached to the Imperial Guards Division broke into the building in hopes of seizing the recording. After a brief skirmish their last-ditch attempt to prevent Japan's surrender was suppressed by loyalist troops, and at noon the people of Japan were stunned to hear, for the first time, the strained high-pitched voice of Emperor Shōwa speaking in the stilted language of the court.

Shōwa carefully avoided the word "surrender," saying instead, with calculated vagueness, that "the war situation has developed not necessarily to Japan's advantage." Nevertheless, noting that "the enemy has begun to employ a new and most cruel bomb," his message was clear: Japan would accept the Potsdam Proclamation; the war was over. His only reassurance was that "Having been able to safeguard and maintain the structure of the imperial state, We are always with ye, Our good and loyal subjects...." [70] Later that day the Allies were notified of Japan's surrender. On September 2, Shōwa's representatives officially signed the formal instrument of surrender at a ceremony held on the deck of the U.S.S. *Missouri* in Tokyo bay.

So ended a war which had caused as many as 1,675,000 Japanese army casualties, 429,000 navy casualties, more than 300,000 civilian casualties, and untold numbers of other Asian and Allied casualties. As to why Shōwa had been able to terminate it in 1945, but not prevent it in the first place, in 1941, he explained to Grand Chamberlain Fujita Hisanori, in 1946:

"The Emperor cannot on his own volition interfere or intervene in the jurisdiction for which the ministers of state are responsible." Once the government adopts a given policy, "I have no choice but to approve it whether I desire it or not" and to act any differently "would clearly be destroying the constitution. If Japan were a despotic state, that would be different but as the monarch of a constitutional state it is quite impossible for me to behave in that way." He insisted, "The circumstances at the end of the war were different from those at the beginning." In August 1945, the government was unable to decide between war or peace, so Prime Minister Suzuki had asked him to intervene: "Here for the first time I was offered an opportunity to state my opinion freely, without infringing anyone's field of responsibility or power. Therefore, I stated my convictions, which I had been storing up, and asked them to end the war."[71]

Shōwa, one senses, was invoking high constitutional principles to cloak his own cautiousness and inability to oppose war more forcefully. Yet at the same time his statement was consistent with his long-held self-image as an "organ" of the state whose chief function was to legitimize the government and its policies, whatever the cost. Like Meiji, he had always emphasized the imperative of each institution of government operating under the rule of law within its properly defined sphere of jurisdictional responsibility. But although he doubtless saw his political role in that light, the fact that he had brought the war to an end in 1945 could not erase the earlier part he had played in sanctioning war. It therefore seemed highly probable that the Allies would try him for war crimes once the Occupation was in place.

Reprieve: Emperor Shōwa and the Occupation

Many leading Japanese expected Shōwa to abdicate in favor of Crown Prince Akihito immediately after the war. The diary of Prince Higashikuni Naruhiko, who took office as prime minister on August 17, 1945, after the resignation of the Suzuki cabinet, indicates that some members of his government believed that Shōwa should abdicate out of a sense of moral responsibility for the war and, one may presume, for Japan's historic defeat and the collapse of the empire.[72] Prince Konoe, who was a key member of Higashikuni's cabinet and who would soon commit suicide rather than stand trial, felt that Shōwa's abdication and retirement to a Buddhist temple in Kyoto was essential to saving the imperial institution.[73] Others, such as Nanbara Shigeru, the president of Tokyo Imperial University, believed that Shōwa wanted to abdicate in taking moral responsibility for the war. Nanbara stated publicly that while Shōwa could not have prevented the war, for which the cabinet bore political responsibility, "I believe that the Emperor is feeling most deeply the moral and spiritual responsibility to the Imperial Ancestors and to the people of this country for the outbreak of such a big war."[74]

Shōwa did, in fact, wish to abdicate. On one occasion late in the war he had told his brother, Prince Takamatsu, that "the present difficulties of the country were due to my lack of virtue (*futoku*)."[75] Now profoundly discouraged by the war and by the totality of Japan's defeat, in August 1945 he revealed to Kido Kōichi his intention to abdicate and to take all responsibility upon himself rather than see Japanese officers stand trial for war crimes. Kido urged him not to do so, arguing that his abdication would weaken the monarchy and encourage the spirit of republicanism in postwar Japan.[76] But Shōwa still thought he should try and spare Japan's military leaders from trial. Thus when Shōwa, dressed formally in cutaway, striped trousers, and silk hat, met the Supreme Commander for the Allied Powers (SCAP), General Douglas MacArthur, for the first time at the American Embassy on September 27, he allegedly told MacArthur, "I come to you … to offer myself to the judgment of the powers you represent as the one to bear sole responsibility for every political and military decision made and action taken by my people in the conduct of the war."[77]

MacArthur, however, had already decided to retain Shōwa on the throne to legitimize, in Japanese eyes, the Occupation's intended reforms of demilitarization and democratization, which were to be implemented through a policy of indirect rule with the cooperation of the Japanese government. This pragmatic consideration, and fears that if Shōwa were tried for war crimes, the Japanese might rise up in resistance to the Occupation, led to Shōwa's reprieve. Shōwa, though, remained determined to abdicate. In 1948, near the end of the Tokyo war crimes trials, he made this intention known to SCAP, only to be informed through intermediaries that his abdication would not be permitted.[78]

Public opinion in countries which had fought imperial Japan ran strongly in favor of trying Emperor Shōwa for war crimes. To many people in Britain, Australia, the United States, and China, for instance, it was inconceivable that he should not be held responsible for Japan's wartime atrocities. In fact, thus far no evidence has been unearthed to indicate that he knew in advance and approved such atrocities as the Bataan death march in the Philippines, the brutal treatment of Asian laborers and Allied prisoners of war along the Burma-Thailand Railway and in other prison camps, or, for that matter, the "rape of Nanking" in the China Incident and the infamous operations of Unit 731.

Certainly, though, at the very least it would have been logical for the International Military Tribunal for the Far East (or IMTFE, which was modeled on the Nuremberg International Military Tribunal in postwar Germany) to indict Shōwa for his complicity in sanctioning war decisions throughout the prewar and wartime period from 1931. As it was, Shōwa's reprieve had significant consequences which merit brief mention here. To begin with, for the IMTFE (which began its proceedings in Tokyo in May 1946) to convict and execute General Tōjō and six other "Class-A" defendants for "conspiracy to wage war" and for "crimes against humanity" without trying Shōwa as well, was highly anomalous and undermined the legal validity of the Tokyo trials. Sir William Webb of Australia, who presided over the IMTFE, dissented from the Tribunal's judgment for this very reason when the final verdict was announced in November 1948.

Next, the punishment of only a selected minority of Japanese leaders made it easier in future years for the Japanese people to evade the problem of their collective responsibility for going along with the war, if not instigating it; Shōwa's reprieve, as head of state and symbol of the nation, only compounded this problem. Unlike the Germans, it seems that to this day most Japanese have preferred to forget the war and

•
182
•

what it meant in their modern history.

Finally, the fact that MacArthur exonerated Shōwa of war responsibility created the lasting impression that the Americans were "covering up" his alleged war crimes. This has led to many claims in Japan and overseas that Shōwa actively and enthusiastically participated in an "imperial conspiracy" for war, whereas it would seem that at most he was guilty of formally sanctioning war and of not trying harder—of not taking greater risks, however remote the prospects of success—to oppose war, possibly by making full use of the imperial prerogatives ascribed to him in the Meiji constitution. His "crimes" were essentially crimes of omission, not commission.

On the occasion of Shōwa's first, and historic, meeting with MacArthur, he and the General were photographed standing side by side—the tall MacArthur, dressed in khaki with his shirt open at the collar, looking relaxed and confident, and his much shorter visitor, tense and meek. This famous photograph alone suggested that reprieved, Shōwa would be little more than a tool in the hands of the Occupation authorities. The photograph also marks the beginning of Shōwa's remarkable transformation from a wartime "manifest deity" into the symbol of a new, peaceful, and democratic Japan.

This process of transformation included many initiatives to demystify the monarchy. SCAP's "Civil Liberties Directive," issued on October 5, 1945, instructed the Japanese government to eliminate repressive laws, to release political prisoners—including Communists who had actively opposed the monarchy—and to ensure free speech and free political action, including the freedom to criticize the emperor without

EMPERORS OF THE RISING SUN

being subject to the crime of lese majesty. The so-called "Shintō Directive" in December further required the abolition of State Shintō, which had comprised a major bulwark of the emperor cult, the prohibition of Shintō ideology in the schools, and the strict separation of church and state. State patronage of Yasukuni Shrine and other shrines was now forbidden.

In the same vein, Shōwa was required publicly to renounce his divinity, which he did on January 1, 1946, stating that the ties between the emperor and the people "do not depend upon mere legends or myths. They are not predicated on the false conceptions that the emperor is divine and that the Japanese people are superior to other races and fated to rule the world." Shōwa himself was probably pleased to reject the notion that he was a god, since he had never personally believed it. But he later acknowledged that his reference in this same statement to Meiji's Charter Oath had been particularly important to him at the time, as a native Japanese basis for democracy and as an antidote to prevailing "radical tendencies" in postwar Japanese society. In commenting on Shōwa's New Year's message MacArthur praised his commitment to democracy. Some foreign observers, though, including the journalist Mark Gayn, were skeptical that the Charter Oath had much to do with genuine democracy.[79] Even so, by publicly renouncing his supposed divinity, Shōwa had taken another step in his descent from "above the clouds."

During the Occupation Shōwa also met with Japanese and foreign journalists for the first time in his career. Although these interviews were carefully orchestrated to prevent any questions on the issue of war responsibility, they did help to demystify him by making him increasingly accessible to the people, who could now, for instance, read about his daily routine in the imperial library, where he and Empress Nagako lived until they moved into the new Fukiage palace upon its completion in November 1961.

The Japanese media also reported Shōwa's many extensive tours, which, prompted by SCAP, did even more to convey him as a "human emperor" (*ningen tennō*), close to the people. Beginning in June 1946, these tours by train or car took him to nearly every part of Japan. Accompanied by court officials (and usually a representative of SCAP), he visited local government offices, factories, mines, schools, hospitals, department stores, sporting events, and so forth, much as Meiji had done on his famous circuits many years earlier. Shōwa did his best, but usually the most he managed to say, when conversing with local hosts, was "*ah sō desu ka,*" like his father at the Taishō Exhibition.

To foreign observers like Gayn, Shōwa looked very ordinary and even pathetic. After Gayn first saw "Charlie," as reporters liked to call Shōwa, during his tour of Saitama Prefecture in March 1946, Gayn wrote that Hirohito

is a little man, about five feet two inches in height, in a badly cut gray striped suit, with trousers a couple of inches too short. He has a pronounced facial tic, and his right shoulder twitches constantly.... He was obviously excited and ill at ease and uncertain of what to do with his arms and hands."[80]

Nevertheless, the Japanese people were very eager to see

Shōwa. In Saitama for example, Gayn looked on as a "dense, silent crowd" suddenly "surged down from the rubble and closed around the emperor," weeping hysterically.[81] Perhaps they saw in Shōwa a father-figure, a symbol of their own survival in hard times. Then, too, they may have been drawn to him by his very awkwardness and physical frailty, for as one Occupation official writes, "Instead of turning on him with fiery disillusionment, they now seemed anxious to mother him and protect him from the world."[82]

There were, of course, many Japanese who had suffered too much in the war not to despise Shōwa intensely. One woman said, "I think [Shōwa] is a hateful person since it was because of him that I ... lost my husband in the fighting and my children in the bombing." A war veteran echoed this sentiment: "I lost my leg in action. My neighbor, an old woman whose son was killed in the war ... told me that nothing could ever erase her hatred for [Shōwa], not even if she could kill him." On the other hand, there was still a powerful residual respect for Shōwa: "he is like a national flag, a form of our existence," or "I do not think that the emperor began or is responsible for the past war.... I feel very sympathetic toward him, for his task is very difficult these days and sometimes I think he wishes that he did not occupy his position."[83] As early as February 1946, one prominent leader of the revived, and now legal, Japanese Communist Party conceded that because "The respect of the people for the emperor is a definite fact," the Party would have to distinguish its demand for the abolition of the monarchy from its comments on the emperor and his family.[84]

In 1948 the strength of popular support for the emperor

prompted the Australian, New Zealand, and Russian representatives on the Far Eastern Commission (an international body based in Washington to monitor the Occupation) openly to complain that his rehabilitation had gone much too far and that it threatened to bring about the revival of the "emperor system." In response, SCAP suspended Shōwa's remaining tours that year to Kyushu, Shikoku, and Hokkaido. But they were resumed in 1949, and Crown Prince Akihito likewise began to appear more frequently in public. His American tutor, Elizabeth Gray Vining, a Philadelphia Quaker whom Shōwa had appointed to teach English to Akihito, commented that wherever the crown prince went, "the crowds gathered.... He was learning fast that an imperial prince belongs not to himself but to the public, and that the privacy and freedom which his humblest subject takes for granted is a precious possession denied to him."[85]

Shōwa's promotion as a "human emperor" unfolded in the context of constitutional reform which SCAP regarded as absolutely fundamental to the democratization of Japan. Dissatisfied with a new draft constitution prepared by the Japanese government, a special committee of SCAP officials worked hurriedly to produce their own draft, and presented it to the Japanese authorities on February 13, 1946, with the strong implication—actually a bluff—that if they did not adopt it as a model, Emperor Shōwa might yet be tried as a war criminal. The Japanese quickly complied but were shocked by its sweeping revisions of the Meiji constitution. Yoshida Shigeru, who later dominated Japanese politics as prime minister (he held office, with several brief interruptions, from May 1946 to December 1954), recalled that "It was only because ... the

Emperor had himself expressed the view that there was nothing in it to which exception should be taken that we brought ourselves to accept" the SCAP draft.[86]

The new constitution, which Shōwa promulgated on November 3, 1946 (technically as an amendment to the Meiji constitution), took effect on May 3, 1947. In brief, besides guaranteeing basic human rights it provided for responsible elected government on the Westminster model, with the Diet as the highest organ of the state. Article nine, which was a quid pro quo for maintaining the monarchy, renounces "war as a sovereign right of the nation" and prohibits the maintenance of "land, sea, and air forces, as well as other war potential." Above all, for our purposes, article one created what many Japanese refer to as the "symbol emperor" (shōchō tennō): "The Emperor shall be the symbol of the state and of the unity of the people, deriving his position from the will of the people with whom resides sovereign power." The emperor was now stripped of all political authority and entirely divorced from government. All of his functions were purely ceremonial and subject to the approval of the cabinet or the Diet. His prerogative of supreme command was eliminated, along with the armed forces.

While the draft constitution was being debated in the Diet, conservative MPs tried to cling to the old order by proclaiming, among other things: "Through the adoption of this Constitution, the Emperor will become a symbol *above* the people...."[87] SCAP immediately rejected this implication of imperial supremacy: "the imperial institution is no longer the source of any authority whatsover, can exercise no powers, and is certainly not indestructible." MacArthur also emphasized pointedly, "In his new role the Emperor will symbolize the repository of state authority—the citizen."[88]

Although, as noted, Shōwa endorsed the new constitution, he did have reservations on various points of constitutional revision. During privy council deliberations concerning parallel changes to the imperial house law he made it known through his younger brother Prince Mikasa that he wished to retain his powers to amend the imperial house law. In the event, however, these powers were transferred to the Diet. He likewise wished descendants of court nobles to be exempt from the abolition of the peerage, but here, too, his views were ignored.[89]

On the more crucial issue of his new status as "symbol emperor," Shōwa seems to have welcomed this change as an appropriate definition of his role as constitutional monarch. Sir George Sansom, the respected English historian of Japan, rightly said of Shōwa, "if the Imperial House can transform itself into a genuine constitutional monarchy on the British model, its continuance will suit our interests. The present Emperor seems anxious to bring about this change...."[90] In most respects Shōwa adapted quickly to this new role, just as Meiji had adapted in Japan's first transition to constitutional government.

Yet like Meiji, Shōwa did not want to be completely marginalized. He still expected to be consulted by ministers of state and to warn and encourage them, as he had done in the past. When he was not consulted, as increasingly was the case during the Occupation and thereafter, Shōwa objected. But as Prime Minister Ashida Hitoshi (in office March–October 1948) said:

It would be harmful for both the imperial family and the nation as a whole if His Majesty gave the impression that he was still meddling in domestic administration and foreign affairs even after the enforcement of the new Constitution. It is for this reason that I refrain from visiting the palace to make informal reports.[91]

Shōwa's opportunities informally to influence the government's decisions had mostly ended. Perhaps to compensate for this, he persistently tried to influence the Occupation whenever he had a chance, especially as the Occupation began its so-called "reverse course" in late 1947. Whereas demilitarization and democratization had been its chief priorities, the situation changed with the escalation of the Cold War in Asia and Europe, the "loss of China" to the Communists in the 1949 Chinese Revolution, and the outbreak in June 1950 of the Korean War. Now the Occupation concentrated on rebuilding the Japanese economy while encouraging Japan's rearmament. This last initiative resulted in the creation of a National Police Reserve and later, in July 1954, the Self-Defense Forces (Jieitai), combining Japanese military, naval, and air units under the administrative authority of a new defense agency attached to the prime minister's office.

The topic of Japanese national security was Shōwa's chief concern in private discussions with MacArthur until April 1951, when President Truman dismissed the general after MacArthur had criticized Washington's strategy of a limited (non-nuclear) Korean war in his capacity as commander of United Nations forces in Korea. Early in 1951 Shōwa also discussed security issues with American Secretary of State John

Foster Dulles in Tokyo, and again with MacArthur's successor, General Matthew Ridgway, in spring 1952. Ridgway later commented that Shōwa "was deeply pleased, he said, at my assurance that the war in Korea could, and would, be brought to a satisfactory close." Moreover, "He said he was delighted that the U.S. had seen fit to send troops to protect northern Hokkaido. I told him that we considered the security of Japan intimately related to our own."[92] By then the U.S.–Japan Security Treaty had been signed (on September 8, 1951), along with the Treaty of San Francisco, which established peace with Japan and officially terminated the Occupation as of April 28, 1952.

However, these and other private attempts by Shōwa to influence U.S. policy were inconsequential, for the Yoshida cabinet had taken full charge of defense matters in negotiations with the United States. Accordingly, as the Occupation drew to a close, Shōwa found himself politically sidelined. This, one would think, was no bad thing for an emperor whose prewar and wartime political career had been so stormy. Moreover, although devoid of political significance, the role of "symbol emperor" was more than he might have expected after escaping retribution at the hands of the Allies. Yet, as Japan headed into a future of unprecedented peace and prosperity, Emperor Shōwa himself would find it quite impossible to escape the realities of the recent past.

Emperor Shōwa Since the Occupation

For the rest of his career Shōwa concentrated on performing his ceremonial constitutional duties. He signed laws, ordinances, treaties, and documents attesting the appointment of

Japanese diplomats and recognizing the diplomatic creden-
tials of foreign envoys to Japan. He presided over receptions
and banquets at the palace and received foreign heads of state
as if he were Japan's head of state, although in fact the constitution did not ascribe this role to him. And he proudly offici-
ated at such occasions as the opening of the Tokyo Olympics
in 1964. The games, held in gleaming new facilities, epito-
mized Japan's rapid economic recovery, followed by high-
speed growth, from the ruins of war.

As during the Occupation, the process continued of "selling" Shōwa to the people as a "human emperor" who personified the adaptation of the imperial house to postwar Japanese
democracy. Through a mass media (including television, from
1953) eager to capitalize on the public's curiosity, the imperial
household agency (formerly the imperial household ministry)
portrayed Shōwa—with no little contrivance—as a rather ordinary, middle class, family man. Newspapers and popular
magazines reported his personal habits in great detail, reveal-
ing, for example, that he typically arose at seven in the morning, ate toast with jam and butter for breakfast, and then,
after a day crowded with official functions, enjoyed playing
parlor games with his family or watching the news, sumō
wrestling, and soap dramas on television. In addition, he was
often photographed admiring the cherry blossoms in the
palace gardens or intently bending over a microscope in his
laboratory, as if to illustrate the compatibility of the monarchy with both the aesthetics of traditional Japan and the scientific and technological spirit of contemporary Japan. When
Crown Prince Akihito dined every week at the palace, father
and son discussed their mutual interest in science; Akihito had

become especially interested in ichthyology.

In one of his New Year's poems, composed in 1966, Shōwa wrote that he wished to learn from the people:

> Would that the wise voice
> Of the man in the street
> Spoke daily to guide us,
> That we might do no wrong
> In performing our duties.[93]

But Shōwa was just too patrician, socially awkward, and too much associated with the war to be projected convincingly as, in effect, the "people's emperor." Postwar Japanese public opinion polls consistently reflected a high level of popular affection, and indeed reverence, towards him, as well as strong support for the imperial institution as a whole. But as time passed they also reflected rising levels of indifference. By contrast, Crown Prince Akihito was much easier to popularize as the symbol of a "new Japan" because he was young and untainted by the violence of his father's early reign. Akihito's increasing appeal to the growing middle class recalled Crown Prince Hirohito's similar appeal, in the 1920s, when he was portayed as the "young Prince."

Akihito emerged in the spotlight of media attention at the time of his coming of age ceremony and investiture in 1952. But he first became a full-fledged media "star" in 1959 when, on April 10, he married a commoner, Miss Shōda Michiko, following their romantic meeting on a tennis court at Karuizawa two years earlier. To many Japanese they were a "dream couple." He was a handsome prince, she, the beautiful daughter of a businessman. The crown princess also quickly became the focus of a "Michiko boom," not unlike the "Diana boom" that later flourished in Britain after Prince Charles married Diana Spencer.

Akihito's many trips overseas, beginning with his attendance as Shōwa's representative at the coronation of Queen Elizabeth II in London in 1953, were detailed by the Japanese media. By 1989, when he became the 125th emperor of Japan, he had represented Shōwa on goodwill missions to thirty-seven countries. Many of them, such as Britain, Sweden, Norway, Denmark, Jordan, Saudi Arabia, Thailand, and Iran (prior to the 1979 revolution) had monarchies with which the Japanese court was keen to maintain close relations.

Akihito often toured Japan as well. But his domestic tours sometimes led to irate protests, as when, accompanied by the crown princess, he visited Okinawa to open the Okinawa Oceanic Exposition in 1975. While the large crowds on hand were mostly enthusiastic, a minority defied heavy police protection to protest that he represented an emperor whom they blamed for the war and especially for the wartime sufferings of the people of Okinawa. Several milk bottles thrown from a building narrowly missed his car as it passed by, and when he and the crown princess honored the war dead at the Himeyuri Monument, a Molotov cocktail was thrown in their direction, but without causing harm. At the same time in Tokyo, the police seized four left-wing activists who had broken into the palace grounds to protest the crown prince's trip to Okinawa.[94]

Plainly, the real target in this instance, and many others like it, was Emperor Shōwa. That was very clear when Shōwa himself visited Hiroshima in April 1971: the city was swept by massive demonstrations protesting the revival of the "emperor system" and its historical associations with Japanese militarism. Despite all the efforts to project him as a democratic "symbol emperor," Shōwa remained a highly controversial figure in postwar Japan.

In part, this was simply because he was still there, a living continuity with the wartime past. But what perpetuated his association with the war even more was the sustained campaign by the Liberal Democratic Party (LDP)—which after its formation in 1955 held power for the rest of the Shōwa period—to rehabilitate imperial sub-symbols of Japanese nationalism which to many Japanese were strongly redolent of the prewar and wartime emperor cult. Behind this endeavor was the LDP's perceived need, in the highly polarized political context of the Cold War, to combat the forces of the left wing, led by the Japanese Communist and Socialist movements. In brief, the LDP sought to build a new modern spirit of nationalism based on respect for traditional social values and institutions, including above all the monarchy, that would appeal to the party's principal supporters, the majority of relatively conservative rural voters and big business.[95]

Over the postwar years the LDP tried to make it obligatory in the schools to honor the flag and sing "Kimi ga yo" on national festival days, and it regularly submitted bills in the Diet to restore state patronage for Yasukuni Shrine, arguing that Yasukuni was a non-religious "cultural asset" which was eligible to receive public funds. In support of this objective, prime ministers made it a practice to visit Yasukuni on August 15 every year. They went in a private capacity until Nakasone Yasuhiro, who held office from 1982 to

EMPERORS OF THE RISING SUN

1987, became the first to do so officially.

These controverial initiatives and others convinced the Japanese left that the LDP was undermining postwar Japanese democracy by turning the clock back to a time when the Hi no Maru flag, "Kimi ga yo," and Yasukuni Shrine were all major elements in the early Shōwa emperor cult. The Communist and Socialist parties succeeded in resisting the restoration of these particular symbols during the Shōwa period, although in 1990 the ministry of education finally made it mandatory to display the flag and sing "Kimi ga yo" on national days in the school calendar. The issue of Yasukuni Shrine still remains controversial today, but no more so than in 1978 when it was revealed that Yasukuni officials had decided to enshrine Tōjō's spirit. This only strengthened memories of the link between Emperor Shōwa, whom Tōjō had served, Yasukuni, and the war.

The same kind of symbolic linkage was evident in the LDP's earlier restoration of Kigensetsu in 1966. That year a bill was passed in the Diet after much debate reviving Kigensetsu under a new name, Kenkoku Kinenbi, or National Founding Day, which would be observed annually on the same date as Kigensetsu, February 11. The prewar past was also echoed in the postwar present when in 1979 the Diet legalized the hitherto customary use of imperial reign names, again over the objections of the opposition.

Shōwa himself was not directly involved in the LDP's efforts to polish and project these old symbols of the monarchy, and it is unknown how he personally regarded these initiatives. But what matters is that because he had been inextricably linked with Yasukuni, Kigensetsu, and so forth in the

•

196

•

prewar and wartime emperor cult, the government's promotion of their revival perpetuated his powerful association with the war. This inevitably made him even more controversial in postwar politics than he otherwise might have been had the government not persisted in its attempted reappropriation of the "symbol emperor" for neo-nationalist purposes. In short, Shōwa was still stigmatized by a past which he had personally hoped to leave behind.

The government was no less keen to transcend the prewar past with one hand even as it perpetuated memories of that past with the other. To illustrate, it used the nation's commemoration of the Meiji centennial in 1966 to highlight Japan's historical progress from feudalism to the present, with scarcely a mention of the wars Japan had fought in its quest for wealth and power. Referring to the importance of honoring the emperor in this national success story, a ministry of education document stated bluntly: "The feelings of respect and love for the Emperor are indissolubly related to the feelings of respect and love for Japan. In other words, to respect and love the Emperor, the symbol of the Japanese state, is to respect and love the state of Japan."[96]

The government's attempts to transcend the past intensified as Japan, which was fast becoming an economic superpower, increasingly engaged in trade wars with America during the 1970s and 1980s. LDP leaders deemed it essential that the Japanese shed their postwar dependency upon America and awaken to the reality that Japan was becoming a major power in international affairs. This is what Prime Minister Nakasone meant when he stressed the imperative of "settling the accounts of postwar politics." Believing that this required a repudiation of the Tokyo trials view of Japanese history, according to which Japan had been the aggressor, some members of his cabinet went so far as to assert publicly that the "Rape of Nanking" was nothing but a figment of Western and Chinese imaginations. For this Japan was vehemently criticized overseas, especially by China. But such denials were nothing new. For years the ministry of education had intervened to alter history textbooks so that, for instance, Japan's invasion of China became a strategic "advance." Other instances of Japanese aggression were deleted altogether.

However, the LDP could not erase the past and nor could Shōwa distance himself from the past. He often tried to do so, by expressing his personal sorrows for what had happened in the war and his pride in Japan's postwar recovery. This was his theme, for example, in a public speech he gave during the nation's government-sponsored celebrations of his sixtieth year in office in 1986. Shōwa said:

> In these sixty years, when all is said and done, the most abominable thing was World War II. What pleased me the most was the splendid recovery after the war, through the efforts of the people, which built the prosperity we know today…. As I contemplate here the sixty years of Shōwa and think of the sacrifices of the people in the last war I am grieved and again feel a reverence for peace.[97]

He probably knew, however, that he would never completely distance himself from the war. That had been painfully obvious when he toured Europe in 1971.

•

•

His return to Britain and the European continent that year was arranged by Prime Minister Satō Eisaku. Satō hoped the tour would help to create a favorable environment for the expansion of Japanese trade with Europe in the wake of the so-called "Nixon shocks," which included economic sanctions against rising Japanese exports to the United States, as well as Nixon's announced trip to the People's Republic of China. In England, however, although the Queen extended a warm welcome to Shōwa, and although he was received into the Fellowship of the Royal Society and reinstated as an honorary field marshal in the British army, a tree he planted in Kew Gardens to symbolize Anglo-Japanese friendship was chopped down and its roots saturated with hydrochloric acid, in a gesture of protest against Japan's wartime brutality towards British prisoners of war. The British press, meanwhile, complained that he did not use the occasion of his visit to apologize for the war.

On the continent Shōwa was again greeted politely by heads of state, but as in Britain, his tour touched off protests wherever he went. In Denmark, feces were thrown at him, and in the Netherlands a bottle was thrown at his car, smashing the windshield. In Germany he was hit by tomatoes and confronted with placards, one of which read, "Hitler killed six million Jews while he [Shōwa] killed fifty million Asians." That his public speeches, which were written by foreign ministry officials, contained no apology whatsoever for the war, again offended many Europeans.

After Shōwa returned to Japan, foreign journalists asked him in an interview about his role in the war. He answered,

In this country my grandfather Meiji established constitutional government and I have acted with the
wishes of Meiji ... as a constitutional monarch. I acted
in that way during the war and at other times. I have
heard comments about my role but there are many
things I really did not know personally.[98]

Shōwa's remarks were scarcely convincing to an international audience that did not know this had been how he had
interpreted his role from the time he ascended the throne. Nor
could his explanation compensate for Japanese atrocities in
former European colonies, the loss of which was still a matter
of profound regret, especially in the Netherlands. Accordingly, at his funeral in January 1989, the Netherlands was represented by Foreign Minister Hans van den Broek, not by a
member of the Dutch royal family. Queen Elizabeth sent
Prince Philip to represent her, but only over the protests of
British servicemen who had suffered terribly in Japanese
prison camps. When Prince Philip came up to Shōwa's casket,
he barely nodded in paying his respects.

Shōwa was given another opportunity to confront, and
transcend, the past when, at the invitation of the American
government, he visited the U.S. in 1975, from September 30 to
October 13. In a prior interview with Bernard Krisher of
Newsweek who asked him about the war, Shōwa explained
again that he had not been able to prevent war in 1941 because
it had been his constitutional duty to sanction the legal decisions of the government, but that when the government was
hopelessly deadlocked in August 1945, he had ended the conflict expressly at Prime Minister Suzuki's invitation. Sum-

ming up his career, he said "The saddest time, without doubt, was the last war."[99]

Shōwa's American tour began controversially. After arriving at Williamsburg, Virginia, his schedule did not include a visit to MacArthur's grave in nearby Norfolk. When instead the Japanese consul general in Atlanta was delegated to lay a wreath on Shōwa's behalf, the General's widow later protested by refusing to attend the banquet given for Shōwa in Washington. She was only partly mollified when Shōwa subsequently went to her hotel in New York to pay his respects. The rest of the tour went well, particularly after Shōwa apologized for the war in a return toast to President Gerald Ford during the aforemontioned Washington banquet, which was held at Smithsonian Castle. His exact words, which had been carefully written by Japanese Embassy officials, came at the end of a general expression of gratitude to the American people for assisting Japan's postwar reconstruction "immediately following that most unfortunate war, which I deeply deplore."

This apology, though muted, was sufficient to placate American feelings, and with the apology behind him, Shōwa came across in most American press coverage as a stooped, gray-haired old man who enjoyed his visit to the Wood's Hole Oceanographic Institute and Marine Biological Laboratory in Massachusetts, where he paused to study marine specimens through a microscope. He was photographed smiling broadly when invited to ride a tractor on a farm in Illinois. His delight was equally apparent when he toured Disneyland with Mickey Mouse and Donald Duck in tow.

On the way home from Hawaii, his plane avoided a route over Pearl Harbor. But upon returning to Japan Shōwa still

•

•

could not avoid questions about the war which his trip had prompted. During a televised interview with Japanese journalists he was asked whether his apology in the United States signified an acceptance of war responsibility on his part. He replied vaguely: "As for the subtle nuances of my remark, not being a specialist in things literary, I am afraid they are beyond me. I am not really able to respond to your question." His answer to another question about the fate of Hiroshima was weak as well. He said he regretted the atomic bomb, "But in the midst of a war, and however tragic it may have been for the citizens of Hiroshima, I believe it was unavoidable." Afterwards, he wondered aloud to court officials, "whether I said enough?"[100]

Shōwa had seemed confused and weary of fielding questions about the past. In a poll taken of people who witnessed the interview on television, twenty-one percent said his performance had been "pathetic;" presumably, many who responded in these terms thought he had been unacceptably nonchalant concerning the atomic bomb victims. A fairly low forty-two per cent said it had made them feel "affection" for him and six per cent professed hostility. Significantly, most of the rest (nineteen per cent) expressed various feelings of indifference.[101]

This indifference grew stronger near the end of Shōwa's reign. A NHK survey in June 1988 recorded that twenty-two percent of those polled felt "favorably" toward him, with another twenty-eight percent saying they felt "affection." But a relatively high forty-seven percent indicated that the strongest emotion Shōwa evoked was "indifference."[102] Newspaper polls conducted three years earlier indicated that over one-third of those polled said they were indifferent toward the imperial institution. This scarcely bore out Nakasone's claim in 1986 that "ninety-nine percent" of the people strongly supported the monarchy. On the contrary, it would appear that despite the government's long-running attempts to enhance public respect for the imperial institution and its many sub-symbols, the monarchy was increasingly viewed as an ornamental irrelevance by the majority of Japanese who were born after the war and who were preoccupied simply with getting on in a highly competitive materialistic society.

To be sure, the news in 1987 that Shōwa was very ill occasioned considerable public concern. The first sign of his decline was in August, when he vomited blood after eating. In September he underwent intestinal bypass surgery (the public was told he was suffering from chronic pancreatitis). As the crown prince took over Shōwa's official duties, Shōwa's health seemed to improve, but in September 1988 he again vomited blood and henceforth had to depend upon massive blood transfusions to stay alive. At this point a mood of "self-restraint" (jishuku) arose in Japan; shoppers stayed home, weddings were canceled, and so forth. By the end of the year over six million Japanese had signed get-well books (kichō) that had been made available. Finally, when Shōwa died of duodenal cancer early in the morning on January 7, 1989, at the age of eighty-seven, large crowds gathered at the imperial palace plaza to pay their respects. Company employees and government officials wore black armbands as a sign of mourning.

But how genuine was this outward grief? It has been suggested that much of it was due to pressure to conform. It has even been said that companies used Shōwa's death as an occasion to strengthen discipline among their employees.[103] Then, too, many young people who cared little about Shōwa's death preferred to watch videos instead of the eulogies that now predominated on television. A newspaper poll conducted in early February revealed that fifty-seven percent of the respondents accused the media of overselling Emperor Shōwa. Only twenty-eight percent felt that the nation's grief for him was genuine.[104] The government of Prime Minister Takeshita Noboru was criticized for using Shōwa's death to divert attention from the "Recruit Scandal."

Representatives of 164 countries gathered in Tokyo for Shōwa's funeral service on February 24. Some Japanese, an estimated one hundred thousand, took this opportunity to attend rallies around the city, denouncing Shōwa as a fascist war criminal. But two hundred thousand people lined the streets on that cold rainy day to watch the funeral procession make its way, accompanied by the sound of bamboo flutes, gongs, and drums, to the Shinjuku Imperial Gardens where the service was held, comprising both a Shintō ceremony (which Communist and Socialist leaders boycotted) and a secular state ceremony. Afterwards, Shōwa's remains were buried next to Taishō's at the Musashino Imperial Mausoleum.

With Shōwa's death, the question was whether the monarchy in the new era of Heisei ("Achieving Peace") could develop a closer relationship with the people of Japan. The earliest indications were promising. In his first televised statement on January 10, Emperor Akihito, speaking in a more informal and direct style than Shōwa had used, told the people, "I wish to work with all of you to abide by the constitution." Since then, the imperial family have often been in the news, albeit too often for some commentators. In an article published in 1994 and entitled, "Is There Not a Danger of Following in England's Footsteps?," the former diplomat Kase Toshikazu deplored the tendency of the Japanese media to probe into the personal affairs of the imperial family in the same intimate way the English media report on the royal family. While conceding that in England such news may foster public affection for the royal family, Kase holds that in Japan investigative reporting of this kind is objectionable because "historically, for the Japanese people the imperial house has been the object not of affection ... but of reverence."[105]

Whether or not that has always been historically true in Japan, the deeper issue here, which points to what may well be the most important legacy of the late Shōwa monarchy, is the problem of increasing public indifference towards the imperial institution as Japan approaches the new millennium. It is too early to say just how far indifference will affect the Heisei monarchy in the future, but as for Emperor Shōwa, during the fiftieth anniversary commemorations of the end of World War II in 1995, there was much renewed speculation in Japan and overseas concerning the extent of his war-responsibility. This is another reminder that despite his reprieve in the Occupation and the fact that Shōwa continued to reign for forty-four years of peace after World War II, he will always be shadowed by memories of war dating from his first nineteen years in office.

NOTES

PREFACE

1 Including an earlier book of my own, *Emperor Hirohito and Shōwa Japan: A Political Biography* (London and New York: Routledge, 1992).

2 Toku Baelz, ed., *Awakening Japan: The Diary of a German Doctor, Erwin Baelz* (Bloomington and London: Indiana University Press, 1974), p. 395.

3 William Elliot Griffis, *The Mikado: Institution and Person* (Princeton: Princeton University Press, 1915), pp. 86–87.

4 I have not included Akihito's reign in this book because it is too recent for historical study. However, the chapter on Emperor Shōwa discusses Akihito's postwar political emergence as crown prince.

5 Yasuda Hiroshi, "The Modern Emperor System as It Took Shape Before and After the Sino-Japanese War of 1894–5," *Acta Asiatica* No. 59 (1990), p. 40.

6 Han Fei-Tzu, quoted from Herschel Webb, *The Japanese Imperial Institution in the Tokugawa Period* (New York and London: Columbia University Press, 1968), p. 157.

MEIJI (The "Restored" Emperor)

1 Hugh Cortazzi, ed., *Mitford's Japan: The Memoirs and Recollections, 1866–1906, of Algernon Bertram Mitford, the First Lord Redesdale* (London and Dover, New Hampshire: Athlone Press, 1985), pp. 120–21.

2 M. William Steele and Tamiko Ichimata, eds., *Clara's Diary: An Ameri-*

can Girl in Meiji Japan (Tokyo, New York, and London: Kodansha International, 1979), pp. 229–30.

3   Toku Baelz, ed., *Awakening Japan: The Diary of a German Doctor, Erwin Baelz* (Bloomington and London: Indiana University Press, 1974), p. 394.

4   Herschel Webb, *The Japanese Imperial Institution in the Tokugawa Period* (New York: Columbia University Press, 1968), p. 122.

5   Sidney Devere Brown and Akiko Hirota, translators, *The Diary of Kido Takayoshi*, 3 vols. (Tokyo: University of Tokyo Press, 1983–86), 1 (1983): 125.

6   Ibid., p.134.

7   For a recent study of Saigō see Charles L. Yates, *Saigō Takamori: The Man Behind the Myth* (London and New York: Kegan Paul International, 1995).

8   Sakamoto Kazuto, *Itō Hirobumi to Meiji kokka keisei: "kyūchū" no seidoka to rikkensei no donyū* (Tokyo: Yoshikawa Kobunkan, 1991), p. 284–86.

9   Brown and Hirota, *The Diary of Kido Takayoshi*, 3 (1986): 204.

10   Ibid., p. 467.

11   Ibid., p. 325.

12   Ibid., p. 333.

13   Donald H. Shively, "Motoda Eifu: Confucian Lecturer to the Meiji Emperor," in David S. Nivison and Arthur F. Wright, eds., *Confucianism in Action* (Stanford: Stanford University Press, 1959), p. 310.

14   Interestingly, Kōmei, Meiji's father, had also opposed Western influences in Japan, just as he had opposed the signing of treaties with the Western powers. Note that Itō eventually relinquished the post of imperial household minister in 1887 on the grounds that to serve concurrently as prime minister and imperial household minister jeopardized the autonomy of the court from the government.

15   William Elliot Griffis, *The Mikado: Institution and Person* (Princeton: Princeton University Press, 1915), p. 145.

16   Mikiso Hane, translator and editor, *Emperor Hirohito and His Chief*

Aide-De-Camp: The Honjō Diary, 1933–36 (Tokyo: University of Tokyo Press, 1982), pp. 194–95; Honjō Shigeru, *Honjō nikki* (Tokyo: Hara Shobo, 1975), pp. 257–58. Meiji had agreed with Russian officials that he would take personal responsibility for the crown prince's safety in Japan. For an interesting contemporary Western account of the Ōtsu Incident, see Hugh Cortazzi, ed., *A Diplomat's Wife in Japan: Sketches at the Turn of the Century* (Tokyo and New York: Weatherhill, 1982), pp. 282–89.

17 Shively, p. 333.

18 Ibid.

19 Baelz, *Awakening Japan*, p. 80.

20 Steele and Ichimata, *Clara's Diary*, p. 86.

21 Bōjō Toshinaga, *Kyūchū gojūnen* (Tokyo: Meitoku Shuppankai, 1960), p. 14.

22 Baelz, *Awakening Japan*, p. 395.

23 Ian Nish, "Sir Claude and Lady Ethel MacDonald," in Ian Nish, ed., *Britain and Japan: Biographical Portraits* (Folkestone, Kent: Japan Library, 1994), p. 144.

24 Brown and Hirota, *The Diary of Kido Takayoshi*, 3: 375.

25 Baelz, *Awakening Japan*, p. 325.

26 Ninagawa Arata, *Meiji tennō* (Tokyo: Sanichi Shobo, 1956), pp. 24–25.

27 Brown and Hirota, *The Diary of Kido Takayoshi*, 3: 423.

28 Kimura Ki, *Meiji tennō* (Tokyo: Waseda Daigaku Shuppanbu, 1964), p. 151.

29 Bōjō, *Kyūchū gojūnen*, p. 34.

30 Watanabe Ikujirō, *Meiji tennō no seitoku, sōron* (Tokyo: Chigura Shobo, 1942), p. 314.

31 Baelz, *Awakening Japan*, p. 97.

32 Joseph Pittau, *Political Thought in Early Meiji Japan, 1868–1889* (Cambridge, Mass.: Harvard University Press, 1967), p. 228.

33 Kunaicho, ed., *Meiji tennō ki*, 13 vols. (Tokyo: Yoshikawa Kobunkan, 1968–77), 7 (1972): 720–23, and Richard T. Chang, "General Grant's

1879 Visit to Japan," *Monumenta Nipponica* XXIV, 4 (1969), p. 384.

34 Chang, p. 365.

35 George Akita, *Foundations of Constitutional Government in Modern Japan, 1868–1900* (Cambridge, Mass.: Harvard University Press, 1967), pp. 42–45.

36 Sakamoto, *Itō Hirobumi to Meiji kokka*, pp. 287–97; also see Osawa Hiroaki, "Emperor Versus Army Leaders: The 'Complications' Incident of 1886," *Acta Asiatica* No. 59 (1990), pp. 1–17.

37 Sakamoto, *Itō Hirobumi to Meiji kokka*, p. 166.

38 Ibid., pp. 173–81.

39 Itō Hirobumi Monjo Kenkyukai, eds., *Itō Hirobumi kankei monjo*, 9 vols. (Tokyo: Hanawa Shobo, 1973–81), 2 (1974): 159.

40 *Meiji tennō ki*, 7: 61–62.

41 Ibid., p. 95.

42 Sakata Yoshio, *Tennō shinsei: Meijiki no tennōkan* (Tokyo: Shibunkaku, 1984), pp. 95–97.

43 Masuda Tomoko, "The Emperor's Right of Supreme Command as Exercised up to 1930: A Study Based Especially on the Takarabe and Kuratomi Diaries," *Acta Asiatica* No. 59 (1990), p. 79.

44 Cortazzi, *A Diplomat's Wife in Japan*, pp. 220–21.

45 *Meiji tennō ki*, 7: 471.

46 Roger F. Hackett, *Yamagata Aritomo in the Rise of Modern Japan* (Cambridge, Mass.: Harvard University Press, 1971), p. 199.

47 Tsuda Shigemaro, *Meiji seijō to Shin Takayuki* (Tokyo: Jishokai, 1928), p. 758.

48 Akita, *Foundations of Constitutional Government*, pp. 110, 121.

49 Tsuda, *Meiji seijō*, pp. 727–28.

50 *Meiji tennō ki*, 9 (1973): 119–20.

51 Sakata, *Tennō shinsei*, pp. 178–79.

52 Kuno Osamu, "The Meiji State, Minponshugi, and Ultranationalism," in J. V. Koschmann, ed., *Authority and the Individual in Japan*

(Tokyo: University of Tokyo Press, 1978), p. 63.

53 Hugh Cortazzi, ed., *Victorians in Japan: In and Around the Treaty Ports* (London and Atlantic Highlands, New Jersey: Athlone Press, 1987), p. 322.

54 Steele and Ichimata, *Clara's Diary*, pp. 206–7.

55 Griffis, *The Mikado*, p. 218.

56 Cortazzi, *Victorians in Japan*, p. 124.

57 Hilary Conroy, *The Japanese Seizure of Korea, 1868–1910: A Study of Realism and Idealism in International Relations* (Philadelphia: University of Pennsylvania Press, 1960), pp. 242–43.

58 *Meiji tennō ki*, 8 (1973): 456.

59 Ibid., pp. 481–82; Stewart Lone, *Japan's First Modern War: Army and Society in the Conflict with China, 1894–95* (London: Macmillan, 1994), p. 85.

60 Lone, *Japan's First Modern War*, p. 31.

61 *Meiji tennō ki,* 8: 511–12.

62 Baelz, *Awakening Japan,* p. 116.

63 Lone, *Japan's First Modern War*, p. 85.

64 Ibid.

65 *Meiji tennō ki*, 8: 809.

66 Ibid., pp. 810–11.

67 Ibid., p. 902.

68 Ibid., 9: 373–74.

69 Ibid., 10 (1974): 158–60.

70 Ian Nish, *The Origins of the Russo-Japanese War* (London and New York: Longman, 1985), p. 9.

71 Shumpei Okamoto, *The Japanese Oligarchy and the Russo-Japanese War* (New York and London: Columbia University Press, 1970), pp. 76–77.

72 Yale C. Maxon, *Control of Japanese Foreign Policy: A Study of Civil-Military Rivalry, 1930–1945* (Westport, Connecticut: Greenwood, 1975 edition), footnote 111, p. 234.

73 Another Japanese source states that during this conference Meiji offered to telegraph the Tsar, in hopes of persuading the Russian government to accept Japan's position on Korea and other matters. The idea, however, was opposed by those present as futile. Cf. Okamoto, *The Japanese Oligarchy*, footnote 160, p. 258.

74 *Meiji tennō ki,* 10: 874–75.

75 For a study of the Japanese Red Cross, see Olive Checkland, *Humanitarianism and the Emperor's Japan, 1877–1977* (London: Macmillan, 1994).

76 Okamoto, *The Japanese Oligarchy*, p. 212.

77 This account of developments in Korea is based on Peter Duus, *The Abacus and the Sword: The Japanese Penetration of Korea, 1895–1910* (Berkeley: University of California Press, 1995), pp. 203–11. Note that as Duus points out, Kojong had changed his title to "emperor" in 1897 (p. 128).

78 Suyama Yukio, *Tennō to guntai (Meiji hen): 'taitei' e no michi to Nisshin nichiro sensō* (Tokyo: Fuyo Shobo, 1985), p. 281.

79 Conroy, *The Japanese Seizure of Korea*, p. 437.

80 *Meiji tennō ki*, 12 (1975): 459–63.

81 Hackett, *Yamagata Aritomo*, p. 156.

82 Roger F. Hackett, Chapter VII "The Meiji Leaders and Modernization: The Case of Yamagata Aritomo," in Marius B. Jansen, ed., *Changing Japanese Attitudes Toward Modernization* (Princeton: Princeton University Press, 1965), pp. 260–61.

83 Cortazzi, *Mitford's Japan*, p. 202.

84 Watanabe Ikujirō, *Meiji tennō no hohitsu no hitobito* (Tokyo: Chigura Shobo, 1938), pp. 282–85.

85 *Meiji tennō ki*, 12: 80.

86 Ibid., pp. 814–15.

87 F. S. G. Piggott, *Broken Thread: An Autobiography* (London: Gale and Polden, 1950), p. 79.

88 Carol Gluck, *Japan's Modern Myths: Ideology in the Late Meiji Period* (Princeton: Princeton University Press, 1985), p. 220.

89 Hackett, *Yamagata Aritomo*, p. 246.

90 Piggott, *Broken Thread*, p. 79.

91 Mochizuki Kotarō, ed., *Sekai ni okeru Meiji tennō*, 2 vols. (Tokyo: Hara Shobo, 1969), 1: 40–41, 58, 174.

92 Griffis, *The Mikado*, pp. 288–89.

93 Gluck, *Japan's Modern Myths*, p. 93. In addition to Gluck's discussion, the best source on the Meiji imperial cult is T. Fujitani, *Splendid Monarchy: Power and Pageantry in Modern Japan* (Berkeley and London: University of California Press, 1996).

94 A. Morgan Young, *Japan Under Taishō Tennō* (London: George Allen and Unwin, 1928), p. 328.

TAISHŌ (The "Retired" Emperor)

1 Jerrold M. Packard, *Sons of Heaven: A Portrait of the Japanese Monarchy* (London: Queen Anne Press, 1988), pp. 226–27.

2 Toku Baelz, ed., *Awakening Japan: The Diary of a German Doctor, Erwin Baelz* (Bloomington and London: Indiana University Press, 1974), p. 125.

3 Kunaicho, ed., *Meiji tennō ki*, 13 vols. (Tokyo: Yoshikawa Kobunkan, 1968–77), 11 (1975): 807. The political context of Yoshihito's trip to Korea was explained in Chapter 1.

4 Takagi Hachitarō and Kojima Tokuhiro, eds., *Taishō tennō gojisei shi* (Tokyo: Kyobunsha, 1927), pp. 15–16.

5 *Taishō nyūsu jiten*, 8 vols. (Tokyo: Mainichi Komyunikeshonzu, 1986), 1: 471–72.

6 Ibid., 2: 546.

7 Hara Keiichirō, ed., *Hara Kei nikki* [hereafter, *HKN*], 6 vols. (Tokyo: Fukumura Shuppan Kabushiki Kaisha, 1965–67), 3 (1965): 245.

8 Ian Nish, Chapter 11, "Sir Claude and Lady Ethel MacDonald," in Ian Nish, ed., *Britain and Japan: Biographical Portraits* (Folkestone, Kent: Japan Library, 1994), p. 142.

•

•

9 Baelz, *Awakening Japan*, p. 146.

10 Ibid., p. 120.

11 Ibid., pp. 389–90, and *HKN*, 3: 276.

12 Osanaga Kanroji, *Hirohito: An Intimate Portrait of the Japanese Emperor* (Los Angeles: Gateway, 1975), p. 21.

13 Takagi and Kojima, eds., *Taishō tennō gojisei shi*, p. 4.

14 *HKN*, 3: 403.

15 Bōjō Toshinaga, *Kyūchū gojūnen* (Tokyo: Meitoku Shuppansha, 1960), p. 65.

16 Nashimoto Itsuko, *Sandai no tennō to watakushi* (Tokyo: Kodansha, 1975), p. 202.

17 Takagi and Kojima, *Taishō tennō gojisei shi*, p. 596.

18 Ibid., pp. 592–93.

19 Baelz, *Awakening Japan*, p. 124.

20 Ibid., p. 363.

21 Honjō Shigeru, *Honjō nikki* (Tokyo: Hara Shobo, 1975), p. 185.

22 Toshiaki Kawahara, *Hirohito and His Times: A Japanese Perspective* (Tokyo and New York: Kodansha International, 1990), p. 43.

23 Takagi and Kojima, *Taishō tennō gojisei shi*, p. 587.

24 *HKN*, 3: 351.

25 Takagi and Kojima, *Taishō tennō gojisei shi*, p. 603.

26 Nashimoto, *Sandai no tennō*, p. 202.

27 Bōjō, *Kyūchū gojūnen*, p. 70.

28 Packard, *Sons of Heaven*, p. 236.

29 Takie Sugiyama Lebra, *Above the Clouds: Status Culture of the Modern Japanese Nobility* (Berkeley and Oxford: University of California Press, 1992), p. 307.

30 *HKN*, 4 (1965): 222.

31 A. Morgan Young, *Japan Under Taishō Tennō, 1912–26* (London: George Allen and Unwin, 1928), p. 18.

32 Ritsumeikan Daigaku Saionji Kinmochi Den Hensen Iinkai, eds., *Saionji Kinmochi den*, 4 vols. (Tokyo: Iwanami Shoten, 1990–96), 3 (1993): 173–87.

33 *Taishō nyusu jiten*, 1: 462.

34 Yosaburō Takekoshi, *Prince Saionji* (Kyoto: Ritsumeikan University, 1933), p. 252.

35 R. L. Sims, *A Political History of Modern Japan, 1868–1952* (New Delhi: Vikas Publishing House, 1991), p. 132.

36 *HKN*, 4: 6.

37 Ibid., p. 30.

38 Ibid., p. 121 and p. 166.

39 Ibid., p. 124.

40 For instance, see Ibid., p. 135.

41 Itō Takashi, ed., *Taishō shoki Yamagata Aritomo danwa hikki* (Tokyo: Yamakawa Shuppansha, 1988), pp. 124–41 gives an especially interesting account of these events from Yamagata's perspective.

42 Shufu no Tomosha, eds., *Teimei Kōgō* (Tokyo: Shufu no Tomosha, 1971), p. 98.

43 Takagi and Kojima, *Taishō tennō gojisei shi*, pp. 595–96.

44 *Teimei kōgō*, pp. 97–98.

45 It was not until October 1922 that Japanese troops, who were the last to go, were withdrawn from Siberia. For a good account of the Siberian Intervention, see James W. Morley, *The Japanese Thrust into Siberia, 1918* (New York: Columbia University Press, 1957).

46 *Saionji Kinmochi den*, 3: 236.

47 *HKN*, 5 (1967): 9.

48 Roger F. Hackett, *Yamagata Aritomo in the Rise of Modern Japan, 1838–1922* (Cambridge, Mass.: Harvard University Press, 1971), p. 319.

49 *HKN*, 5: 166. It was decided that Prime Minister Hara would substitute for Taishō in formally opening the Diet for fear that if his subjects saw the extent of Taishō's disabilities, there might be a widespread crisis of confidence in the monarchy; cf. Tanaka Nobumasa, *Taishō tennō*

no "taiso": "kokka gyōji" no shūhen de (Tokyo: Dai-san Shokan, 1988), pp. 9–10.

50 Minami Hiroshi, *Taishō bunka* (Tokyo: Keiso Shobo, 1965), p. 224. This is not to deny that owing to the continuing institutional charisma of the imperial house Taishō was still held in high esteem by many Japanese even after the regency came into being. In 1923 a rare public opinion poll of 3,500 factory workers in Tokyo revealed that for 793 Taishō was the greatest figure they could think of, ahead of even Emperor Meiji and the Buddha. See Nakamura Masanori, "Senzen tennōsei to sengo tennōsei," in Rekishigaku Kenkyukai, eds., *Tennō to tennōsei o kangaeru* (Tokyo: Aoki Shoten, 1986), pp. 128–29.

51 *HKN*, 5: 279–80.

52 Lesley Connors, *The Emperor's Adviser: Saionji Kinmochi and Pre-war Japanese Politics* (London: Croom Helm, 1987), p. 216.

53 *HKN*, 5: 249.

54 The texts of these medical reports are found in Tanaka, *Taishō tennō*, beginning with the first report on pp. 3–4.

55 Itō Takashi and Hirose Yoshihiro, eds., *Makino Nobuaki nikki* (Tokyo: Chūō Kōronsha, 1990), p. 20.

56 Shikama Kōsuke, *Jijū bukan nikki* (Tokyo: Fuyo Shobo, 1980), p. 271.

57 Packard, *Sons of Heaven*, p. 246.

58 Hackett, *Yamagata Aritomo*, pp. 339–40.

59 Stuart Kirby, *Japan and East Asia: Documentary Analyses, 1921–1945* (London and New York: I.B. Tauris Publishers, 1995), p. 98.

60 Kojima Noboru, *Tennō*, 4 vols. (Tokyo: Bungei Shunjū, 1981), 1: 226–28; Shikama, *Jijū bukan nikki*, pp. 277–79.

61 *HKN*, 5: 385.

62 Shikama, *Jijū bukan nikki*, p. 283.

63 Connors, *The Emperor's Adviser*, p. 88.

64 Oka Yoshitake and Hayashi Shigeru, eds., *Taishō demokurashī ki no seiji: Matsumoto Gokichi seiji nisshi* (Tokyo: Iwanami Shoten, 1977), p. 162.

NOTES

65 Young, *Japan Under Taishō Tennō*, p. 298. Note that the emperor and empress were in Nikkō at the time of the earthquake.

66 Taishō Shuppan Kabushiki Kaisha, eds., *Shinbun shūroku Taishō shi* [hereafter, SSTS], 15 vols. (Tokyo: Taishō Shuppan, 1978), 11: 545–47.

67 *HKN*, 5: 408.

68 Kanroji, *Hirohito*, p. 90.

69 *SSTS*, 9: 348.

70 He went with heavy police protection, for in the lawless aftermath of the earthquake crowds of people went around beating up and killing Koreans who were suspected, quite absurdly, of poisoning the wells and other such deeds; in another violent episode, a military police officer also murdered the well-known anarchist Ōsugi Sakae, his wife Itō Naoe, and Ōsugi's nephew, who was only a boy.

71 Young, *Japan Under Taishō Tennō*, p. 309.

72 *SSTS*, 12: 204–5.

73 This problem was solved with the birth of the present Emperor Akihito on December 23, 1933. In all, Emperor Shōwa and Empress Nagako had five daughters, beginning with Princess Shigeko, and one other son besides Akihito, Prince Yoshi-no-miya Masahito (or Hitachi), who was born in November 1935.

74 Richard J. Smethurst, *A Social Basis for Prewar Japanese Militarism: The Army and the Rural Community* (Berkeley, Los Angeles, and London: University of California Press, 1974), p. 164; italics added.

75 *SSTS*, 13: 215.

76 Tanaka, *Taishō tennō*, pp. 34–74.

77 Nakajima Michio, *Tennō no daigawari to kokumin* (Tokyo: Aoki Shoten, 1990), pp. 26–28.

78 These efforts to control public behavior are detailed in Tanaka, *Taishō tennō no "taiso,"* pp. 54–56 and pp. 246–48.

79 Kirby, *Japan and East Asia*, p. 117. The diary of Kawai Yahachi, a senior imperial household ministry official, is especially informative concerning the government's systematic orchestration of these events marking the Taishō-Shōwa ritual transition. See Takahashi Hiroshi,

Awaya Kentaro, and Otabe Yuji, eds., *Shōwa shoki no tennō to kyūchū*, 6 vols. (Tokyo: Iwanami Shoten, 1993–94), Vol. 1 (1993).

80 Carol Gluck, *Japan's Modern Myths: Ideology in the Late Meiji Period* (Princeton: Princeton University Press, 1985), p. 83.

SHŌWA (The "Reprieved" Emperor)

1 Inoue Kiyoshi, *Tennō no sensō sekinin* (Tokyo: Gendai Hyōrōnsha, 1975), p. 84.

2 Osanaga Kanroji, *Hirohito: An Intimate Portrait of the Japanese Emperor* (Los Angeles: Gateway, 1975), p. 23.

3 HRH The Duke of Windsor, *A King's Story* (London: Cassell, 1951), pp. 179–80.

4 Toku Baelz, ed., *Awakening Japan: The Diary of a German Doctor, Erwin Baelz* (Bloomington and London: Indiana University Press, 1974), p. 363.

5 Kanroji, *Hirohito*, p. 16.

6 Kojima Noboru, *Tennō*, 4 vols. (Tokyo: Bungei Shunjū, 1981), 2: 58.

7 Quoted from a *Time* magazine interview, October 6, 1975, p. 42.

8 Otake Shuichi, *Tennō no gakkō* (Tokyo: Bungei Shunjū, 1986), p. 228.

9 Leonard Mosely, *Hirohito: Emperor of Japan* (Englewood Cliffs, New Jersey: Prentice-Hall, 1966), pp. 70–71.

10 Kanroji, *Hirohito*, p. 60.

11 Honjō Shigeru, *Honjō nikki* (Tokyo: Hara Shobo, 1975), p. 254–55.

12 Ibid., p. 241.

13 Ibid., p. 185.

14 Kanroji, *Hirohito,* p. 58.

15 This world view, drawn from scientific Darwinism, made it possible for Hirohito and other like-minded Japanese to believe that knowledge, broadly construed, was the means to the "suvival of the fittest" in the harshly competitive "dog eat dog" world of social Darwinism, as

popularized in Meiji Japan through the works of Herbert Spencer. Sugiura often emphasized to Hirohito that it was to this end—to ensure Japan's progress on the road to wealth and power—that Meiji had proclaimed in the Charter Oath, "Knowledge shall be sought throughout the world."

16 F. S. G. Piggott, *Broken Thread: An Autobiography* (London: Gale and Polden Limited, 1950), p. 128.

17 Mosley, *Hirohito*, p. 57.

18 Date Munekatsu, *Tennō no gaikō* (Tokyo: Gendai Kikakushitsu, 1975), p. 9.

19 It is interesting that Tanner's themes were reported in the special issue of *Fujin gahō*, mentioned in the previous chapter, which typified the detailed media coverage in Japan of Hirohito's European tour.

20 Lesley Connors, *The Emperor's Adviser: Saionji Kinmochi and Pre-war Japanese Politics* (London: Croom Helm, 1987), p. 145.

21 Carol Gluck, *Japan's Modern Myths: Ideology in the Late Meiji Period* (Princeton: Princeton University Press, 1985), p. 237.

22 Yamamoto Shichihei, *Shōwa tennō no kenkyū: sono jitsuzō o saguru* (Tokyo: Shodensha, 1989), p. 19.

23 Charles D. Sheldon, "Japanese Aggression and the Emperor, 1931–1941, From Contemporary Diaries," *Modern Asian Studies* Vol. 10, No. 1 (1976), pp. 37–38.

24 Saionji had served as Japan's chief delegate to the Paris Peace Conference, where he was assisted by Makino and Chinda Sutemi. As Saionji once said, "My duty to the Emperor is twofold, to avoid damaging the spirit of the Constitution and to honor international treaties." Cf. Harada Kumao, *Saionji-kō to seikyoku*, 9 vols. (Tokyo: Iwanami Shoten, 1950–56), 2 (1950): 108.

25 Terasaki Hidenari and Mariko Terasaki Miller, eds., *Shōwa tennō dokuhakuroku—Terasaki Hidenari goyōgakari nikki* [hereafter, STDH] (Tokyo: Bungei Shunjū, 1991), pp. 22–23. This source contains invaluable records of Shōwa's postwar "monologue," which he delivered in five secret meetings to a group of palace officials in March and April 1946. Historians generally agree the purpose was to prepare his defense in the event that he was brought to trial for war crimes.

26 Ibid., p. 23.

27 Harada, *Saionji-kō to seikyoku*, 1 (1950): 85.

28 Honjō, *Honjō nikki*, p. 162–63.

29 Mikiso Hane, translator and editor, *Emperor Hirohito and His Chief Aide-de-Camp: The Honjō Diary, 1933–36*, (Tokyo: University of Tokyo Press, 1982), "Introduction," p. 63.

30 Harada, *Saionji-kō to seikyoku*, 2: 160.

31 Ogata Sadako, *Defiance in Manchuria: The Making of Japanese Foreign Policy, 1931–1932* (Berkeley: University of California Press, 1964), p. 94.

32 Honjō, *Honjō nikki*, p. 189.

33 Hatano Sumio and Kurosawa Fumitaka, eds., "Nara Takeji jijū bukanchō nikki," *Chūō Kōron* (October 1990), p. 348. General Nara was Shōwa's chief aide-de-camp.

34 Harada, *Saionji-kō to seikyoku*, 2: 288.

35 Honjō, *Honjō nikki*, p. 163.

36 Kido Kōichi, *Kido Kōichi nikki*, 2 vols. (Tokyo: Tokyo Daigaku Shuppankai, 1966), 1: 101.

37 Harada, *Saionji-kō to seikyoku*, 2: 115.

38 Kido, *Kido Kōichi nikki*, 1: 127.

39 Joseph Grew, *Ten Years in Japan* (New York: Simon and Schuster, 1944), p. 122.

40 Harada, *Saionji-kō to seikyoku*, 4 (1951): 238.

41 Honjō, *Honjō nikki*, pp. 206, 208.

42 Harada, *Saionji-kō to seikyoku*, 7 (1952): 278–79.

43 Kanroji, *Hirohito*, p. 135. The standard English-language account of the rebellion is Ben-Ami Shillony, *Revolt in Japan: The Young Officers and the February 26, 1936 Incident* (Princeton: Princeton University Press, 1973).

44 Honjō, *Honjō nikki*, p. 275.

45 Ibid., p. 292.

•

46 Irie Sukemasa, "My 50 Years with the Emperor," *Japan Quarterly*, Vol. XXX, No. 1 (1983), pp. 39–40.

47 James B. Crowley, *Japan's Quest for Autonomy: National Security and Foreign Policy 1930–1938* (Princeton: Princeton University Press, 1966), p. 393.

48 Harada, *Saionji-kō to seikyoku*, 6 (1951): 206.

49 Ibid., p. 208.

50 Together with Ishiwara Kanji, Itagaki had orchestrated the Manchurian Incident in 1931. Shōwa had agreed to their subsequent promotion not because he approved of the Manchurian Incident but because he was afraid of offending the army.

51 Harada, *Saionji-kō to seikyoku*, 7: 51.

52 Ibid., pp. 339–40.

53 Sanbo Honbu, eds., *Sugiyama memo: daihon'ei-seifu renraku kaigi hikki*, 2 vols. (Tokyo: Hara Shobo, 1967), 1: 278.

54 *STDH*, p. 52.

55 *Sugiyama memo*, 1: 286.

56 Robert J. C. Butow, *Tōjō and the Coming of the War* (Princeton: Princeton University Press, 1961), pp. 254–55.

57 Ibid., pp. 377–86.

58 *STDH*, pp. 136–37.

59 Suyama Yukio, *Tennō to guntai (Meiji hen): "taitei" e no michi—nisshin nichiro sensō* (Tokyo: Fuyo Shobo, 1985), pp. 291–92.

60 Kido, *Kido Kōichi nikki*, 2: 949.

61 Ibid., p. 945.

62 Hosokawa Morisada, *Jōhō tennō ni tassezu*, 2 vols. (Tokyo: Isobe Shobo, 1953), 1: 43.

63 Higashikuni Naruhiko, *Higashikuni nikki* (Tokyo: Tokuma Shoten, 1968), p. 135. Higashikuni had married one of Taishō's sisters and was thus an uncle of Hirohito's. He was the only imperial prince to serve as prime minister, but only briefly, from August 17, 1945, soon after Japan surrendered, to early October.

64 *STDH*, pp. 100, 102.

65 Kawahara Toshiaki, *Hirohito and His Times: A Japanese Perspective* (Tokyo and New York: Kodansha International, 1990), p. 122.

66 John Dower, *Empire and Aftermath: Yoshida Shigeru and the Japanese Experience, 1878–1954* (Cambridge, Mass.: Harvard University Press), p. 265.

67 *STDH*, pp. 126–27.

68 Robert J. C. Butow, *Japan's Decision to Surrender* (Stanford: Stanford University Press, 1967), pp. 175–76.

69 Ibid., pp. 207–8.

70 Ibid., p. 248.

71 Fujita Hisanori, *Jijūchō no kaisō* (Tokyo: Kodansha, 1961), p. 205.

72 Higashikuni, *Higashikuni nikki*, pp. 235–36.

73 Hata Ikuhiko, "Tennō no shinsho," *Bungei shunjū* (October 1978), p. 376.

74 Ōkubo Genji, *The Problem of the Emperor System in Postwar Japan* (Tokyo: Japan Institute of Pacific Studies, 1948), p. 17.

75 Itō Takashi, et. al., eds., *Tōjō naikaku soridaijin kimitsu kiroku* (Tokyo: Tokyo Daigaku Shuppankai, 1990), p. 130.

76 Kido, *Kido Kōichi nikki*, 2: 1, 230–31.

77 Douglas MacArthur, *Reminiscences* (London: Heinemann, 1965), p. 288.

78 Hata, "Tennō no shinsho," pp. 386–92.

79 Mark Gayn, *Japan Diary* (Rutland, Vermont and Tokyo: Charles E. Tuttle Company, 1981), p. 93.

80 Ibid., p. 137.

81 Ibid., pp. 139–40.

82 Russell Brines, *MacArthur's Japan* (New York and Philadelphia: Lippincott, 1948), p. 84.

83 These quotations, recorded in various public opinion surveys conducted during the Occupation, are found in Hugh H. Smythe and Watanabe Masaharu, "Japanese Popular Attitudes Toward the Em-

peror," *Pacific Affairs* Vol. XXVI, No. 4 (1953), pp. 335–44.

84 Michael P. Hayes, "The Japanese Press and the Emperor, 1945–1946," in Gordon Daniels, ed., *Proceedings of the British Association for Japanese Studies*, Vol. 3, No. 1 (1978), p. 158.

85 Elizabeth Gray Vining, *Windows for the Crown Prince: Akihito of Japan* (Tokyo: Charles E. Tuttle, 1989), p. 121.

86 Yoshida Shigeru, *The Yoshida Memoirs* (Cambridge, Mass: Riverside Press, 1962), p. 137.

87 Gayn, *Japan Diary*, p. 125; italics added.

88 Courtney Whitney, *MacArthur: His Rendezvous with History* (Westport, Conn: Greenwood Press, 1977), p. 285.

89 Besides abolishing the peerage system, SCAP reduced the number of imperial family members; gave the Diet control of appropriations to maintain the imperial household; reduced the vast imperial estate including properties, stocks, and other assets; and replaced the imperial household ministry with the imperial household agency, which is attached to the prime minister's office.

90 Takeda Kiyoko, *The Dual-Image of the Japanese Emperor* (London: Macmillan, 1988), p. 160.

91 Watanabe Osamu, "The Emperor as a 'Symbol' in Postwar Japan," *Asia Asiatica* No. 59 (1990), p. 113.

92 Matthew B. Ridgway, *Soldier: The Memoirs of Matthew B. Ridgway* (New York: Harper, 1956), p. 227.

93 Kanroji, *Hirohito*, p. 150.

94 Takahashi Hiroshi, *Gendai tennōke no kenkyū* (Tokyo: Kodansha, 1978), pp. 270–73.

95 For a more detailed discussion of the LDP's campaign in these postwar decades, see Stephen S. Large, *Emperor Hirohito and Shōwa Japan: A Political Biography* (London and New York: Routledge, 1992), chapters 7 and 8.

96 I. A. Latyshev, "Reactionary Nationalist Tendencies in the Policy of the Ruling Circle of Japan," *Asia Quarterly*, Vol. 1 (1973), p. 11.

97 Hando Kazutoshi, "Shōwa tennō hachijū shichinen no kiseki," *Bungei*

shunjū March, 1989 [Special Issue: Ōinaru Shōwa], p. 459.

98 *The Guardian*, November 17, 1971.

99 "A Talk With the Emperor of Japan," *Newsweek*, September 29, 1975, p. 56.

100 Takahashi, *Gendai tennōke no kenkyu*, p. 14.

101 Nishihira Shigeki, "Tennō, nengo, kokka, kokki," *Jiyū* Vol. 22, No. 1 (1980), p. 86.

102 Ishida Takeshi, "The Emperor Problem in a Historical Perspective," in Yoshikazu Sakamoto, ed., *Prime* [International Peace Research Institute Occasional Papers, Meiji Gakuin University], No. 5 (1989), p. 47.

103 Watanabe Osamu, "The Sociology of *jishuku* and *kichō*: The Death of the Shōwa Tennō as Reflection of the Structure of Contemporary Japanese Society," *Japan Forum* Vol. 1, No. 2 (1989), pp. 279–87.

104 Yoshikazu Sakamoto, "Introduction: The Essence of the Problem," in Yoshikazu Sakamoto, ed., *Prime*, No. 5 (1989), p. 17.

105 Kase Toshikazu, "Eikoku no tetsu o fumu kiken wa nai ka," *Bungei shunjū* Vol. 72, No. 1 (January 1994), p. 127. Kase's point, that media coverage of the royal family fosters public affection for the English monarchy, is increasingly belied by growing signs today of public cynicism and disillusionment caused by the well-known matrimonial problems within the wider royal family.

INDEX

Numbers in bold indicate entire chapters.